A Mapmaker's Diary

A Mapmaker's Diary

Selected Poems

Carlota Caulfield

Translated by Mary G. Berg
in collaboration with the author

White Pine Press / Buffalo, New York

White Pine Press
P.O. Box 236
Buffalo, New York 14201
www.whitepine.org

Acknowledgments: This book includes poems selected from Carlota Caulfield's collections *Autorretrato en ojo ajeno* (Betania, 2001), *Movimientos metálicos para juguetes abandonados* (Primer Premio Hispanoamericano de Poesía "Dulce María Loynaz" 2002. La Laguna, Tenerife: Gobierno de Canarias, 2003), *The Book of Giulio Camillo (a model for a theater of memory) / El Libro de Giulio Camillo (maqueta para un teatro de la memoria)*, (InteliBooks, 2003), and *Quincunce / Quincunx* (Book Supplememt of *Puerto del Sol,* 2004), and a selection of new poems from *Islario General* (unpublished). Acknowledgments are due to the editors of the following publications in which some of the new poems first appeared: *Caribe: Revista de Cultura y Literatura, Hostos Review, Walrus* and *Decir del agua.*

Publication of this book was made possible, in part, by a Women's Studies Quigley Summer Grant from Mills College, and with public funds from the New York State Council on the Arts, a State Agency.

First Edition.

Cover Painting: Diego Rodríguez de Silva y Velázquez, *Female Figure (Sibyl with Tabula Rasa)*, c. 1648. Used by permission of Meadows Museum, SMU, Dallas. Algur H. Meadows Collection, MM.74.01.

ISBN: 978-1-83996-88-5

Printed and bound in the United States of America.

Library of Congress Control Number: 2007937844

In memory of my grandfather
Edward Henry Caulfield de Pons

Contents

Prologue / 11

Carlota Caulfield, Poet in Transit by Aimée G. Bolaños / 15

from *Autorretrato en ojo ajeno/Self-portrait in Another's Eye* (2001)

Con mi rueca / 22
With My Distaff / 23
Jan Vermeer Van Delft desenfoca su pintura por un temblor de tierra / 24
Jan Vermeer Van Delft's Painting Slips Out of Focus
Due to an Earthquake / 25
Autorretrato en un espejo convexo / 26
Self-portrait in a Convex Mirror / 27
Aureo ojo el origen / 28
Golden Eye the Origin / 29
Dame la mano, que voy con argénteo paso / 30
Give Me Your Hand, For I Go with Silvery Tread / 31
Tres poemas que hablan de la anatomía de un mago / 32
Three Poems That Speak of a Magician's Anatomy / 35
Desde una ventana de San Francisco / 38
From a Window in San Francisco / 39
Sombras chinescas / 40
Chinese Shadows / 41
Templo de epigramas / 42
Temple of Epigrams / 43
El peor dibujo del triángulo / 44
The Worst Drawing of the Triangle / 45
En el contexto del canto / 46
In the Context of the Song / 47
Calles de México D.F., 1994 / 48
Streets of Mexico City, 1994 / 49

Elegía desde New Orleans / 50
Elegy from New Orleans / 52

from *Movimientos metálicos para juguetes abandonados*
Metallic Movements for Abandoned Toys (2002)

Londres, cualquier día / 56
London, Any Day / 58
Quantum Corral / 60
Quantum Corral / 61
"I remember, yes, I remember" / 62
"I remember, yes, I remember" / 63
Rue de la Messine 10 / 64
Rue de la Messine 10 / 66
Cuatro cuentos chinos / 68
Four Chinese Stories / 71
Para Sabina, In Memoriam / 74
For Sabina, In Memoriam / 76
La Poésie est comme lui / 78
La Poésie est comme lui / 79
Raimundus Lullus se pasea de la mano de Heather Davis
por los jardínes del archiduque Luis Salvador / 80
Raimundus Lullus Goes Walking Hand in Hand with Heather Davis
Through the Gardens of Archduke Luis Salvador / 81
Bitácora / 82
Binnacle / 83
After Virgilius Bononiensis
(vista de pájaro de la ciudad de Amberes en 1565) / 84
After Virgilius Bononiensis
(A Bird's Eye View of the City of Antwerp in 1565) / 85
Plantin-Moretus / 86
Plantin-Moretus / 87
Les cages sont toujours imaginaires / 88

Les cages sont toujours imaginaires / 90
Movimientos metálicos para juguetes abandonados / 92
Metallic Movements for Abandoned Toys / 93

from *El Libro de Giulio Camillo (Maqueta para un teatro de la memoria)*
The Book of Giulio Camillo (A Model for a Theater of Memory) (2003)

El Libro de Giulio Camillo / 96
The Book of Giulio Camillo / 97

from *Quincunce*
Quincunx (2004)

Por la viva inquietud de la ciudad / 104
Through the Alert Restlessness of the City / 110
Oquedad del caracol (soplo divino) / 116
Inner Chamber of the Seashell (Divine Whisper) / 121
En la ansiedad de mi ojo, una súbita cesación del tiempo / 126
In the Anxiety of My Eye, Time Suddenly Stops / 132

from *Islario General*
Compendium of All the World's Islands
(unpublished)

Amach, el maestro Zen y confidente sin par
de una poeta llamada Carlota Caulfield / 140
Amach, the Zen Master and Unrivaled Confidant
of a Poet Named Carlota Caulfield / 142
Luisa Futoransky y la gravedad / 144
Luisa Futoransky and Gravity / 145
De formas aerodinámicas y espejos de navegantes / 146

Of Aerodynamic Shapes and Navigators' Mirrors / 149

Other books by Carlota Caulfield / 153
The Author / 155
The Translator / 156

Prologue

Carlota Caulfield might be defined as a verbal acrobat, a juggler of words and images, a magician of memory. This present anthology, *A Mapmaker's Diary,* gathers recent poems, both published and unpublished, by this Cuban-born writer who has lived in the U.S. for the last twenty five years. The poems of *A Mapmaker's Diary* center on travel, on what it means to be perpetually in transit, and what it means to live in a Western society in this era of rapid and kaleidoscopic change. The poems' narrative voices are ever in motion, ever curious, constantly redefining themselves, trying on new identities as they journey restlessly between cities and between centuries in Caulfield's omnivorous rereadings of cultural texts and pictorial images. Caulfield writes passionately about a wide range of urban centers, artists and texts, in explorations ranging from Leonardo da Vinci's flying machines to Remedios Varo's images of traveling women.

As in her eleven previous books of poetry, Caulfield reflects (as in multiple self-reflecting and inter-reflecting mirrors) her own life experiences that began in Havana just before the Cuban Revolution, and her meditations on the enduring icons and urban centers of Western culture as she has moved from Havana to Zürich to New York, New Orleans, and San Francisco. The poems explore her interconnections with London, Dublin, Barcelona, and many other cities she loves. As she writes in "In the Anxiety of My Eye, Time Suddenly Stops:"

There are cities that sow a little madness
in the minds of their inhabitants, and all that has not been possible
in other places, through strange occult forces finds propitious terrain there.
There are cities with skies like magic lanterns
Havana, Dublin, Barcelona, Palma de Mallorca, Zürich, Las Cruces,
New Orleans and Prague perforate pupils and are inhabited by sinister
demons that pursue the solitary.

The poems in this bilingual anthology, translated into English by Mary G. Berg in collaboration with the author, are united in their awareness (and interrogation) of what defines identity, of what impels human beings to be curious about the world, and the multiple forms that this curiosity assumes. Carlota Caulfield feels herself to be both an insider and an outsider as she visits cities and texts: she travels with a powerful sense of her own personal life and yet with her eyes open to new and strange experiences. She journeys through ancient mythic cities, populated by beasts and memories of "obliterated texts," seeking (in her meditation on Theseus in "Temple of Epigrams"):

> ...a voice that's lost
> in labyrinths, in canals,
> in a sea that changes...

lamenting that

> ...No labyrinth gives us clues
> that allow us to decipher
> where we are and who we are.

Often she is an anonymous traveler, "a watchful eye that travels quietly," alert to the implications and interconnections of all she beholds, fascinated by the texts and images of antiquity, imagining the speculations of (among others) Chinese emperors, of Prospero, of the 11th century Irish King Suibne of Ros Earcain, of Leonardo thinking of Icarus who yearned to fly and constructed wings only to fall to earth when he flew too close to the sun, of how

Of all the legends of long gone times,

the one about the daring flight, that celebrates the desired person,
and awards no commemorative medal, is the one which announces
that life continues, that innumerable stories have been told
about men who have risen into the air,
that the ability to fly is an attribute of devils or of heretics.

("Of Aerodynamic Shapes and Navigators' Mirrors")

Born into a nomadic family that moved through Ireland and Catalonia, France and Spain, Carlota Caulfield retraces her steps and those of her ancestors. Her memories of her Cuban childhood and family, including her beloved nanny Blasa, are especially emotionally charged because Caulfield left Cuba in 1981 for Zúrich to keep traveling from city to city, describing herself as a wanderer of the "Irish-Catalan-Jewish-Cuban Diaspora," ever a stranger, ever at home in her role as traveler and observer. The poet's personal journey through life has expanded into a fascination with all journeys, quests and memories of the past, journeys through others' memories as well, in paintings and books. Travel, identity and memory are finally indistinguishable, inseparable, and imbued with myth, magic and humor. Although memory may be brief, as Caulfield muses in *The Book of Giulio Camillo,*

> ...the memory of the memory itself
> allowed the hand to retain the word.

[M.G.B.]

Carlota Caulfield, Poet in Transit

Aimeé G. Bolaños*

Carlota Caulfield sets her mirrors to reflect movement in time and space, creating unusually diverse discursive strategies while revealing stage directions on how to read her aesthetics and her textual practices, as when she introduces herself as she travels across London in "London, Any Day," saying that

No one knows anything about me, only that I'm a poet in transit,
that I speak English with a certain indefinable accent,
and that my nationality is cryptic.

Within rich contexts of explicitly fictionalized writing and of authorial presence, Carlota Caulfield's poetics of travel assume particular relevance as the transcultural journey becomes an aesthetic experience with intense spiritual and creative dimensions. Themes of return and nostalgia, of painful memory of loss and grief, familiar to readers of Cuban poetry of the diaspora, appear with heightened meanings. The original culture, at the heart of such productive multicultural contacts, is recreated based on the distinctive personal vision of this poetry. By defining herself as a poet in transit, she is able to circulate through all zones of knowledge and cross between various cultures, situating herself somewhere between where she began and a destination not yet reached.

In this state of in-betweenness, refusing to be either inside or outside, she becomes a truly itinerant being. Her first-person recall is subject to influence and influencing, open to all sorts of experience. She portrays a being composed of memory who weaves her own imaginings into the complex webs of the diaspora.

As they invent places and draw boundaries, Caulfield's texts splice together a single imaginary map of overlayered external and internal worlds. Restoring past phases of existence as she seeks herself, her poems can be cultural transmissions of profound resonance. On center stage is the multicultural space of the journey, location not only of encounters and epiphanies, but of dramatic recollections of experiences of solitude and uprootedness, the emblematic site of the poet's efforts, exile and wanderings.

The creation of herself, which in Caulfield's poetics is also defined as the singular adventure of self-portraiture in another's eye, allows her not only to inhabit other gazes, and from these new perspectives to constitute herself through the other's view, but to reach out to intrinsic otherness, with unsuspected aesthetic and existential implications. Carlota Caulfield's poems are transpersonal and transcultural self-creation. The author interprets variations of the return to herself, recounting how her gaze is also present in the eyes of alterity. At the same time, and recurrently, she assumes the perspective of movement, of literal and symbolic —that is, figural— journeys.

Memory makes these poems into gardens of forking paths, cracks of light that contain the figure of the author, surprised in the act of writing as she inscribes and translates her signs into the book of memory, now also a book that takes on a literal body in the world of life. Eye and word engage in an intense relationship. A result of this interaction is a metaphoric pronouncement of the writing that celebrates the creative power of the gaze and the word, and above all explores language. Because the visual eye is also the analytical eye that configures a vision into language, both the eye and the word indistinguishably constitute object and subject under permanent scrutiny. More than assertive, they are disruptive embodiments of the semiotic order in the symbolic. They open writing to meanings in whose center is found the fabulist nature of the poet registering the fluctuating forms of her dynamic self. Her world is conjectural, one of memory games in shifting art and of permutations. Caulfield's texts operate by association and transformation, and model a reading that occurs in a zone of contacts, shifting sands and exchanges. Thus we as readers can only reconfigure ourselves in transit.

The artistic singularity of Carlota Caulfield's poetic project stands out. The project is almost unclassifiable, although critics tend to label her interconnections as postmodernist aesthetics or even as neo-surrealism. A reader of Ovid, Catullus and Martial, immersed as an author/reader in canonical practices of literary history, who travels in a selective and intimate way, open to heterogenous philosophic, esoteric, mythologic, and historical presences, and to other forms of spiritual culture and diverse forms of art, especially painting, a constant underlayer in her historicist rather than philologizing affiliations. Her work is the result of a process of apprenticeship that allows her to include others' discourses within her own. As a consequence, her knowledge is intersubjective, dialogical and intercultural, assembled as an exercise in freedom in which subversion and ratification go hand in hand.

Carlota Caulfield's identity as a transculturated poet is expressed through transgressive strategies that find their most original expression in rewritings and combinations of styles. Hypertextuality, heterophony, plural discursivity, syncretic genealogies, semblances of liturgies and rituals proliferate in this poetry, announcing it as heterodox and experimental. Like a mobile constructed of language, her poems employ the precise forms of metamorphoses and journeys.

Internal cartography of imagined space, art of a ruminating memory, the poetry of *A Mapmaker's Diary* seems to lead us to a rite of passage which could imbue the interconnectedness of life with rich and contradictory possibilities, as well as the underlying Cuban origin, recontextualized into an expanded network of communications. Transforming absences into rebirths, recuperating primordial signs under other labels, moving in any direction toward the dark radiation of poetry, Carlota Caulfield invites us to the reinvention of ourselves and of our culture, to the flight of memory, to the journey.

[Translated and abridged by Mary G. Berg and Carlota Caulfield]

*Universidade Federal do Rio Grande do Sul, Brazil

Yo soy el único espectador de esta calle,
Si dejara de verla, se moriría.
—Jorge Luis Borges

I am the only spectator of this street.
If I were to stop looking at it, it would disappear.
—Jorge Luis Borges

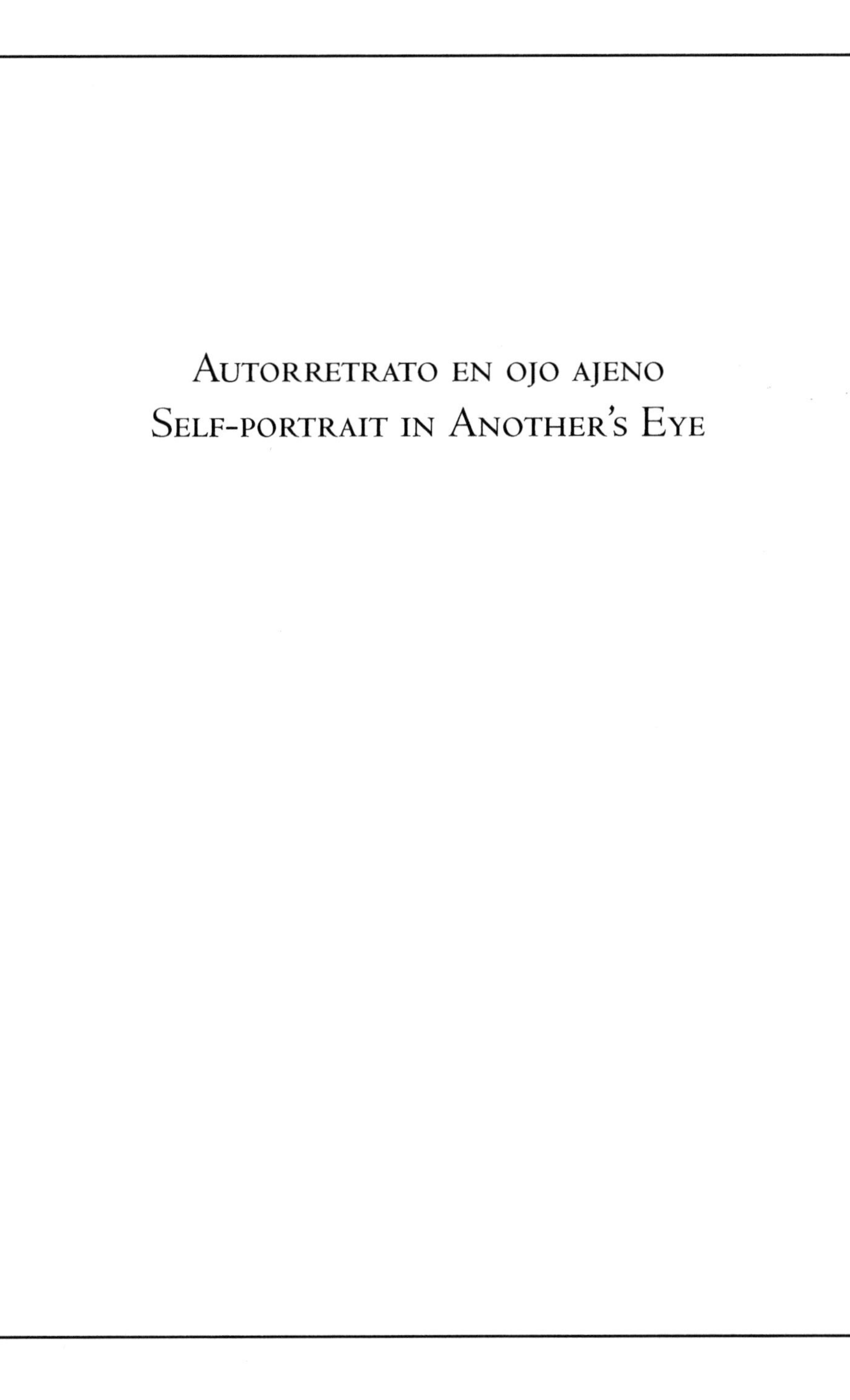

Autorretrato en ojo ajeno
Self-portrait in Another's Eye

Con mi rueca

No reconozco mi color.
En Alejandría perdí mi sombra
y toda apariencia de ciudad
ha sido belleza de lo inútil.
Todas mis coartadas sólo
sirvieron para estrechar
los lazos con la muerte.
Mi cuerpo encuadernado de lino
y la operación final
de enrollar mis venas.

With My Distaff

I don't recognize my color.
In Alexandria I lost my shadow
and all semblance of a city
has been the beauty of the useless.
All my alibis
only served to strengthen
the ties to death.
My body bound in linen
and the final act
of rolling up my veins.

Jan Vermeer Van Delft desenfoca su pintura por un temblor de tierra

Le cerraría a esa tarde el deliro del viaje.
Varado en alta sierra quiere el espacio
considerar el umbral del salón desierto.
En los pasajes sin precisa memoria
las letras se dejan saborear.

Las sombras se descifran y los ojos absorben
las figuras de los cuerpos desnudos. Presentir la
caricia que asciende hacia el centro de la cúpula y
la escritura en su respuesta más simple.
Materia que se abre entre la que observa
y el arco de tus cejas.

El puente levadizo inventa el cuadro.

Jan Vermeer Van Delft's Painting Slips Out of Focus Due to an Earthquake

No travel obsession would obtrude into that afternoon.
Stranded on the high mountainside, space wants
to consider the threshhold of the vacant living room.
In the passages without precise memory
letters let themselves be tasted.

Shadows are deciphered and eyes take in
the outlines of naked bodies. An intuition
of the caress that ascends to the cupola's center
and writing in its simplest answer.
Matter that unfolds between the observer
and the arch of your brows.

The drawbridge invents the painting.

Autorretrato en un espejo convexo

A Paco Jarauta

En el cuadro hay un niño sonámbulo, pero no se puede
saber si camina o vuela. El movimiento de la retina
no quiere terminar el juego de lo que reposa o se alza.
El hilo de luz crea una transparencia en la mano que hace
ver su anillo. Parmigianino es capaz de refractarse.
En el cuadro hay una niña sonámbula,
pero no se puede saber si camina o vuela.

Convergencias. Fluir desde el riesgo de una mañana
anónima. Los niños entran en la cámara lúcida y se
dan la mano. Un día nos veremos al otro lado del
prisma, abriéndonos caminos en territorios lúdicos.

Habítame en ellos.

Self-portrait in a Convex Mirror

To Paco Jarauta

In the painting there's a sleepwalking child, but it's hard
to know whether he's walking or flying. The retina's movement
doesn't want to define the play between resting and rising.
The thread of light creates the hand's transparency, allowing
his ring to be seen. Parmigianino is capable of self-refraction.
In the painting a little girl is sleepwalking,
but there's no way to know if she's walking or flying.

Convergences. Flowing from the risk of an anonymous
morning. Children enter the lucid chamber and reach out their hands
to each other. One day we'll see the prism's other side,
opening our paths through playful territory.

Inhabit me there.

Aureo ojo el origen

Dos amantes caminan por un muro húmedo
y aparece frente a ellos una ciudad.
Suave es el animal que abre su mirar,
disuelve su respiración
y se desnuda entre espacios sin límites.

Una gota de agua fresca trae consigo
un olor a este mismo instante.

Golden Eye the Origin

Two lovers walk along a humid wall
and a city appears before them.
Gentle is the beast who opens his gaze,
dissolves his respiration and strips naked
amidst unlimited spaces.

A drop of fresh water brings with it
an odor at this very instant.

Dame la mano, que voy con argénteo paso

Inquieto caminar de la memoria
que santigua los textos borrados.

Una criatura se inclina
entre la extensión del oído tenaz
y unos labios que triplican la imagen.

Give Me Your Hand, for I Go with Silvery Tread

Restless steps of memory
sanctifying the obliterated texts.

A child bends over
between extending a tenacious ear
and lips that triple the image.

Tres poemas que hablan de la anatomía de un mago

I
ni tanta despedida,
ni tanto mirar,
sólo así.

II
animal de trote
animal de trote en la lluvia que cae en mi rostro.

Tiene una cicatriz en el hombro izquierdo, su piel es como
textura de arándano silvestre, oscura casi violácea, pero
no amarga, sino con dulzor de semen que discurre por mis
venas de rutas desconocidas. Memoria tatuada. Miel y pachulí.
¿Por qué?
No entraste en mí. Bilocación iniciática de hoy
que llueve con rabia y puedo escribir frente a la absoluta
respiración. Ceremonia de risas. Nuestra mutua presencia
que suda
que lame
que estalla (arena)

Frente a los establos la fruta puede ser redonda.
La fruta está a punto cuando se encuentra dura
y rebota en la mesa de la cocina. Me leíste.
Ya lo dice aquí: el cultivo del arándano requiere mucho
trabajo, un clima y terreno especiales y un cuidado tan
exigente que no se recomienda a un aficionado. Pero
no hay mesa de cocina, sino puro paisaje, puro aire.
Ni más palabras, ni más silencios. Sólo una señal.

Llegó a buscarme vestido de negro
no sé de qué color tenía los ojos.

Sólo recuerdo dos cosas:
su boca, grande y sensual,
sus manos, infinitas y luminosas.

El camarero me contaba de su viaje a San Francisco.
Café. Lluvia. Silueta. Mirada.
Celebro el hambre atroz
en mi chaleco de monedas.
Aquello es una salpicadura sobre el espejo del baño.
Labios que se cruzan, se detienen y se devoran.
Lenguas como manos de dioses o cantos.

Un cuerpo contra la puerta de una habitación de hotel.
Un cuerpo contra el espacio de una habitación de hotel.

III
Del piso cuarto al séptimo
hay corrientes de aire.
Ven, que yo te cuento.
Contémonos como la enredadera de arándanos
prospera en tierras arenosas, bajas, y bosques profundos.
Gozo interrumpido. Ciclo de amor cada dos años.
He aprendido muchas cosas de ti que me han gustado.

Te paso una moneda de mi puño a tu puño,
de mi boca a tu boca.
Entonces se fue, ¿quieres que te lo diga?
y me dejó mirándolo.

Las despedidas pueden ser redondas, ovaladas,
en forma de campana o pera, pero la nuestra
es geométricamente hasta pronto.

Te diste una ducha. Leíste. Bajaste a tomar un café. El mago se paró frente a tu mesa. Subiste a tu habitación. Abriste las cortinas. La ciudad de Lexington se humedece frente a ti.

Three Poems That Speak of a Magician's Anatomy

I
neither so many farewells
nor so much gazing
only thus.

II
trotting animal
trotting animal in the rain that falls on my face.

He has a scar on his left shoulder, his skin has the
texture of wild blueberries, dark, almost violet, but
not bitter but with the sweetness of semen that flows through my veins
along unknown routes. Tattooed memory. Honey and fragrant mint.
Why?
You did not enter me. Today's initiatory bilocation
rains anger and I can inscribe it against absolute
respiration. A ceremony of laughter. Our mutual presence
sweating
licking
bursting (sand)

Across from the stables the fruit may be round.
The fruit is ripe when it is hard and bounces
on the kitchen table. You read to me.
It says right here: growing blueberries requires great
effort, special climate and soil, and so much care
that it's not recommended for amateurs. But there's no
kitchen table, only open landscape, open air.
No more words, no more silences. Only a gesture.

He came looking for me dressed in black
I don't know what color his eyes were.
I only remember two things:
his mouth, wide and sensual;
his hands, infinite and luminous.

The waiter told me about his trip to San Francisco.
Coffee. Rain. Profile. Gaze.
I celebrate terrible hunger
in my vest of overlapping coins.
That's a splash on the bathroom mirror.
Lips that cross, stop, and devour each other.
Tongues like the hands of gods or songs.

A body against the door of a hotel room.
A body against the space of a hotel room.

III

From the fourth floor to the seventh
there are currents of air.
Come, I'll tell you about it.
Let's tell each other how the blueberry plant
thrives in low sandy areas and in deep forests.
Uninterrupted pleasure. A love cycle every two years.
I've learned many things from you that I've liked.

I pass you a coin from my fist to yours,
from my mouth to yours.
Then he went away —do you want me to tell you that?—
and he left me gazing after him.

Goodbyes can be round, oval,
bell or pear shaped, but ours

is geometrically see you soon.

You took a shower. You read. You went down for a coffee. The magician stood before your table. You went up to your room. You opened the curtains. The city of Lexington gleams damply before you.

Desde una ventana de San Francisco

Palpitación del hilo rojo
que necesita ser mano,
conciencia y espacio.

No hay opción.
El texto carece de ilustraciones
y el plazo de admisión
depende de un verso de Pessoa
que ironiza sobre la apariencia
como coartada cultural.

From a Window in San Francisco

Throb of the red thread
that must be hand,
conscience and space.

There's no option.
The text lacks illustrations
and the deadline for submitting it
depends on a line from Pessoa
that ironizes about appearance
as cultural alibi.

Sombras chinescas

Hasta el eje sediento de mi centro:
no existe ningún espejo claro.

Chinese Shadows

At the very thirsty core of my being:
no clear mirror exists.

Templo de epigramas

Empujar, golpear en el oído
para que el sonido entre.

Hay una voz que se pierde
en los laberintos, en los canales,
en un mar que cambia, rico y extraño.

Teseo encontró la salida del laberinto,
pero caminó en círculos hasta que sus manos
aplacaron la tormenta de su pulsar eléctrico.

Todo ego exige claridad sobre uno mismo
y el otro. Ningún laberinto nos da signos
por los que podamos descifrar
dónde estamos y quiénes somos.

Temple of Epigrams

Shove, beat on the ear
so that the sound will enter.

There's a voice that's lost
in labyrinths, in canals,
in a sea that changes, rich and strange.

Theseus found the labyrinth's exit,
but he walked in circles until his hands
appeased the torment of his electric beats.

Every ego demands clarity about itself
and the other. No labyrinth gives us clues
that allow us to decipher
where we are and who we are.

El peor dibujo del triángulo

Capacidad figurativa del cuerpo
en su variado signo.

The Worst Drawing of the Triangle

The body's figurative ability
in its varied signs.

En el contexto del canto

Una silueta de hombre engendra sed
en mi memoria como caricia poderosa.
El verano estalla del lado del deseo
y establece un reino
de rumores que discurren entre ausencias.

In the Context of the Song

A man's silhouette causes thirst
in my memory like a powerful caress.
Summer bursts beside desire
and establishes a kingdom
of voices that argue amidst absences.

Calles de México D.F., 1994

Dos veces en la tarde tu imagen filtró el aire.
Mi diario de viaje transitó en espiral
y la fragmentación de la ciudad
se alzó como un pájaro de papel.
Para qué recorrer la vida urbana
si he tenido que decapitarme
en homenaje a un desconocido
(arde la enorme visión
de un anuncio de Coca-Cola).

De todas las voces que descienden por mi cuerpo
la del arquero que me sirve de ojos
ha recorrido un círculo:
bailo alrededor de tu rosa.

Streets of Mexico City, 1994

Twice in the afternoon your image purified the air.
My travel diary spiralled along
and the city's fragmentation
soared like a paper bird.
Why travel around urban life
if I've had to decapitate myself
in honor of an unknown man
(the enormous vision
of a Coca-Cola ad blazes).

Of all the voices that descend upon my body
that of the archer who serves as my eyes
has traced a circle:
I dance around your rose.

Elegía desde New Orleans

Para Artemio, In Memoriam

Calles de San Francisco en la punta de mi lengua,
vasija con canto, con júbilo,
con piel húmeda a la entrada de la casa.
Calles de San Francisco en la noche que tú conocías.
Cada una de nuestras pasiones
era Miguel, y otra vez Miguel,
que se dejaba acariciar entre cita literaria
y los latidos de nuestras venas.
Sin apurarnos. Sin esperar nada.
Mejor que durara así, por mucho tiempo,
para que nos diera todo lo que tenía y aquello
que nos haría indulgentes.

Boca que se ofrece.
Infinito hilo de saliva que nos marca
con suavidades táctiles.

Y después, a cada cual su ciudad.
New Orleans nutrida con aguas.
Y una herida sagrada en sagrado vaso
de niñez urbana, de aguaceros,
y un futuro que no recuerda más.

Fue corta la memoria.
Después los ojos contra cajas de fotografías
y tu historia urdida con saliva en muchas bocas
que me ofreció lo que siempre se agradece:
enseñanza del ojo.

Fresca la ropa se intercambia. Yo juego.
Allí, significa una ciudad en la que dos amigos

hacen un inventario de despedidas,
tocan sus cicatrices, apagan sus olores,
y a cada cual su piel de hilachas.

Mañana significa una ciudad de anfiteatros
y el nombre de Dinócrates tatuado en mi cuello.
Allí, significa ese viaje que se valida
sin itinerarios, del ser herido en sí mismo.

Y ahora, mi memoria se despierta
en papel timbrado, y una llamada de teléfono
que engendra la poderosa sed de un dolor de garganta,
de la travesía por una Sala de Emergencia,
de un malestar donde queda escrita una palabra,
hay una sola que no consigo nombrar.

La noche con fruncida angustia
con ropa fresca que ignora a los muertos
y una perversa lentitud:
piel habitada por hormigas
que en vano se ocultan del cuerpo
en hilachas de grito:
río que pudre sus aguas frente
a un ojo cuidador que viaja tranquilo.

Elegy from New Orleans

For Artemio, in Memoriam

Streets of San Francisco on the tip of my tongue,
vessel with song, with joy,
with damp skin at the house's threshold.
Streets of San Francisco on the night you knew so well.
Each of our passions
was Miguel, and Miguel again,
who let himself be caressed between literary quotes
and the heartbeats of our veins.
Without haste. Without expecting anything.
Better it should have gone on thus, for a long time,
to give us all it held and that
which would make us indulgent.

Mouth that offers itself.
Infinite thread of saliva that marks us
with tactile softnesses.

And afterward, to each his city.
New Orleans nourished by waters.
And a sacred wound in a sacred vessel
of urban childhood, of thunderstorms,
and a future that remembers no more.

Memory was short.
Later on, eyes against boxes of photos
and your history made up of saliva in many mouths
a history that offered me what is always appreciated:
the teachings of the eye.

We exchange clean clothes. I play.
"There" means a city in which two friends

stock an inventory of goodbyes,
touch their scars, stifle their odors,
and to them both their skin of rags.

Tomorrow means a city of amphitheaters
and the name of Dinocrates tattooed on my neck.
"There" means that journey undertaken
without itineraries, within the very wounded self.

And now my memory awakes
on letterhead stationery, and a telephone call
stirs up the powerful thirst of a sore throat,
of your journey through an Emergency Room
of pain where a word is inscribed,
there's only one I cannot name.

The night with furrowed anxiety
with clean clothes that ignore the dead
and a perverse slowness:
skin inhabited by ants
that hide from the body in vain
in ragged shreds of scream:
river that muddies its waters before
a watchful eye that travels quietly.

Movimientos metálicos para juguetes abandonados
Metallic Movements for Abandoned Toys

Londres, cualquier día

Me he paseado por todo Londres
con mi viejo abrigo de cuero negro
y un sombrerito de tela, torcido en los bordes.
De mí nadie sabe nada, sólo que soy una poeta en tránsito,
que hablo inglés con cierto acento indefinido,
y que mi nacionalidad es confusa.
Aunque en Londres me libré de algunos duendes perversos
que me persiguen desde mi nacimiento, se me unieron otros,
quizás el peor de todos sea el que no deja de soplarme al oído
"Regresemos, regresemos pronto, que allí está nuestra vida."

Como no he podido librarme de ese duende insistente,
he releído, aunque con poco entendimiento,
la astrocarta que me hicieron en 1987.
Sí, quizás la voz insistente tenga razón.
En mi mapa del mundo aparece
que Júpiter me favorece en las Islas Británicas,
que debo escaparme a París con un actor galés,
y que moriré en la isla de Menorca.

Pero Londres no termina en la pura especulación ni en el puro ensueño.
Estamos en noviembre y yo vivo en Bloomsbury,
lo que me da cierto regusto literario.
Toda tarjeta postal que envío
se apropia de mis paseos diurnos y de una cierta euforia
casi ya desconocida.
Veinticinco libras esterlinas me dan la llave de la ciudad
desde un autobús de tonos carmelitosos.
Aunque varios guías turísticos me ofrecen
por el mismo precio toda clase de visitas
a museos y paseos en barco,
yo, sin saber por qué, quiero sentarme
en ese autobús,

el menos pintoresco,
y que los ruidos de la ciudad lleguen hasta mí.

Lo que yo quiero es empaparme de arquitecturas y panoramas.
Ver cómo la gente se amontona en los cruces de calles,
cómo los monumentos cambian de forma,
y cómo reúno fuerzas para poder regresar a mi hotel,
cambiarme de ropa en diez minutos y volver a hablar de poesía.

London, Any Day

I've walked all around London
in my old black leather coat
and a little cloth hat, curled up at the edges.
No one knows anything about me, only that I'm a poet in transit,
that I speak English with a certain indefinable accent,
and that my nationality is cryptic.
Although in London I've freed myself from some perverse spirits
that have haunted me since my birth, I've taken on others,
perhaps the worst of which is that little voice that whispers in my ear
"Let's go back, we'd better go back soon, our life is back there."

Since I haven't been able to rid myself of that insistent voice,
I've reread, though not with great understanding,
the astro-chart that was custom-made for me in 1987.
Yes, perhaps the insistent voice is right.
On my map of the heavens it appears
that Jupiter favors me in the British Isles,
that I will run off to Paris with a Welsh actor,
and that I will die on the island of Menorca.

But London doesn't end there in pure speculation or in pure fantasy.
It's November and I'm living in Bloomsbury
which gives me a certain literary thrill.
Every postcard I send
reflects my daily strolls and a certain euphoria
that is almost unheard of these days.
Twenty five pounds sterling give me the key to the city
seen from a caramel-hued bus.
Although various tourist guides offer me
all sorts of museum visits and boat tours
for the same price,
without knowing why, I want to sit
in this bus,

the least picturesque,
where the city noises reach me.

What I want is to immerse myself in architectures and panoramic views,
to see how people crowd together in intersections,
how the monuments change their shapes,
and how I gather the energy to be able to return to my hotel,
change clothes in ten minutes and go back to talking about poetry.

Quantum Corral

En busca de luz llega un viajero a su casa ancestral para mirarse en las aguas de un río. Hoy es el día de Santa Brígida y la herida que desde su nacimiento lleva el viajero, aunque no sana, deja de doler lo suficiente como para lanzarlo a regresar una y otra vez a un montículo de sonidos y de trazos.

Sí, el viajero entra varias veces en una biblioteca (la más amada) y señala con el dedo de la mente todas las cosmografías que contienen el nombre de la ciudad de su padre.

Dublín, noviembre de 1999

Quantum Corral

In search of light, a traveler came to her ancestral home to gaze at herself in the water of a river. Today is Saint Bridget's Day and the wound the traveler has borne since her birth, although it does not heal, becomes sufficiently painless to impel her to return again and again to a jumble of sounds and penstrokes.

Yes, the traveler makes several entries into a library (the best loved one) and points out with her mental finger all the cosmographies that contain the name of her father's city.

Dublin, November 1999

"I remember, yes, I remember"

A Marcello Mastroianni, y a Carmen

Ser arquitecto es el sueño del actor que a los setenta y tres años reflexiona.
Frente al puente de Eiffel y los rascacielos de New York,
la mente goza de esos trajes alusivos que sólo algunos privilegiados conocen.
Sí, dejé la arquitectura por el teatro, pero no dejo de soñar con una casa que
gire en lo alto del más alto edificio. Sí, con una casa que gire en la suavidad
de una caricia. Pocos muebles, algunos libros, entre ellos Stendhal y Chejov,
y la mano amiga y tierna de mi mujer.
Una morada en Roma, otra en París,
la llave del umbral y las tantas risotadas que estallarán
para hacer saltar a los podadores de vida.
Porque he vivido, sí, con alegría y locura, por eso la vida me ha regalado con
saltos inesperados, grandes amores y amigos curiosos.
He sido un hombre frugal,
si dejamos a un lado mis cincuenta cigarros diarios,
¿a quién se le ocurre, no?
En cuanto a lo que han dicho de mí, todo ha sido pura invención de los americanos,
eso de llamarme Latin Lover es en verdad ridículo y hasta poco elegante.
Son tantas las cosas que me gustaría contarles ahora, ahora que soy un viejo real,
no como los viejos de mis películas. He sido lo bastante atrevido como
para hacerme bello y agradar al público, siempre tan exigente.
He sido el arquitecto de paisajes imposibles, y en ellos veo
la belleza de un mundo que ya deja de ser para mí.

(After the film *I remember, yes, I remember,* directed by Anna María Tato, 1997)

"I remember, yes, I remember"

To Marcello Mastroianni, and to Carmen

Becoming an architect is the dream of the actor who reflects at age seventy-three.
As he stands before the Eiffel bridge and New York skyscrapers,
his mind delights in those allusive costumes known only to a few privileged people.
Yes, I left architecture for the theater,
but I've never stopped dreaming of a house that spins
atop the tallest building. Yes, of a house that spins on the softness of a caress.
Not much furniture, a few books, among them Stendhal and Chekhov,
and my wife's familiar and tender hand.
A home in Rome, another in Paris,
the key of the threshold and the many outbursts of laughter
that will startle those who feel uneasy with life.
Because I've lived, yes, with joy and madness, and this is why life has rewarded me
with unforeseen leaps, great loves and unusual friends. I've been a frugal man,
if we leave aside my fifty daily cigarettes,
and who would want to count them, after all?
As for what they've said about me, it was all contrived by the Americans,
that entire tale that labeled me as a Latin Lover is really
ridiculous and not even elegant in fact.
There are so many things I'd like to tell you about now,
now that I've become a genuine old man,
not a bit like the old men in my films. I've always been daring enough
to dress myself up and please the public, always so demanding.
I've been the architect of impossible landscapes, and in them I see
the beauty of a world that now ceases to exist for me.

(After the film *I remember, Yes, I remember,* directed by Anna María Tato, 1997)

Rue de la Messine 10

I

Una miniatura francesa del siglo XIV
representa el espíritu o Ángel de la Juventud,
con alas en los pies.
Vuela sobre el mar
y sus alas están pintadas de verde.
Lleva en sus hombros a un peregrino de mediana edad,
pelo muy corto, nariz aguileña, ojos ¿acaso grises?,
¿sonríe acaso a quienes lo observamos?

Este es mi abuelo Edward Henry Caulfield
una tarde en un París de cielo despejado.

II

Elle ne perd pas le Nord, un globo zeppelin
inscribe letras en el cielo de un París caluroso.
Aimée y yo no hemos encontrado el primer laúd del mundo,
aunque lo hemos buscado minuciosamente, yo en mi
francés infantil, y ella con su suelta lengua belga.
Pero sí hemos descubierto un tesoro arquitectónico y sentimental:
casa de mi abuelo, alta, blanca, huesuda como un animal prehistórico
en buena forma.

Y como yo soy casi especialista en reliquias
y una sentimental casi de telenovela,
me puse a llorar de alegría;
casa, morada, palacio señorial que albergó la diáspora de los míos,
en un París de excepciones y gestos.

Y así la Rue de la Messine, ciudadana y pulida,
deseosa y deseante, abierta, y nosotras
en varias combinaciones.

Rue de la Messine 10

I

A 14th century French miniature
represents the spirit or angel of Youth;
with winged feet.
He flies over the sea
and his wings are painted green.
On his shoulders he carries a middle aged pilgrim,
sharp nose, very short hair, eyes – maybe gray?
Can he be smiling as we stare at him?

This is my grandfather, Edward Henry Caulfield
one afternoon in Paris under a clear sky.

II

Elle ne perd pas le Nord, a zeppelin blimp
sketches letters in the sky over a sweltering Paris.
Aimée and I have not found the world's first lute,
although we've searched everywhere for it, I in my
childhood French, and she with her fluid Belgian tongue.
But we have discovered an architectural and sentimental treasure:
my grandfather's house, tall, white, stark as a prehistoric animal,
preserved.

And since I'm almost a specialist in relics
and as sentimental as a character in a soap opera,
I burst out crying in happiness;
house, dwelling, great palace that sheltered my family's diaspora,
in a Paris of exceptions and of gestures.

And that's the Rue de la Messine, urban and polished,
desired and desiring, open, and we
in various combinations.

Cuatro cuentos chinos

I. Espejo de metal

Un antiguo cuento chino
habla de un tal emperador Ts'in Shi (259-210 A.C.)
que poseía "el precioso espejo que iluminaría los huesos del cuerpo",
también conocido como "el espejo que ilumina la bilis".
El espejo aparece descrito como sigue:
rectangular de cuatro pies de ancho, cinco pies y nueve pulgadas de alto,
brillante tanto en su interior como en su exterior.
Cuando alguien ponía las manos sobre su corazón,
observaba en el espejo sus vísceras.
Cuando un hombre se paraba ante él para ver su reflejo,
su imagen aparecía fragmentada en diminutos círculos.
De acuerdo con otra leyenda, era un pedazo de madera
sacada de un árbol llamado "el rey de los químicos".

II. Papalotes como pájaros

En un comentario de los *Anales de los libros de Bambú*
el emperador chino Shu es descrito como "ser volador",
"primer hombre que descendió sano y salvo en un paracaídas"
y "el que volaba como un pájaro".
Asciendo a la torre y no puedo descender,
mi padre le ha pegado fuego y todo se desploma.
Era el siglo XII.
Gracias a mi buena cabeza y a mis dos sombreros de paja,
sombrillas útiles en cualquier circunstancia,
me tiro y aterrizo en tierra, con mi vestido de hilo en plena forma.
En definitiva, a pesar de las conspiraciones de mis hermanos,
siglos después Leonardo da Vinci me ha dejado trazado
en una de sus muchas libretas de aviación.
Después el veneciano Fausto Veranzio, ¿era acaso el siglo XVI?,

hizo varios trazos arrebatados y modificó el diseño.
Debo aclarar que el verdadero descenso de alguien en un paracaídas
no sucedió hasta 1783 en Montpellier.
Mis conocimientos de geografía son escasos,
y los nombres extranjeros me marean, pero aún así,
debo reconocer que los libros de historia
a veces dicen algunas verdades,
y además, yo estaba allí. En plena forma.

III. Yü min o aquellos que vuelan

Algunos escritores chinos cuentan sobre un país de seres voladores,
una isla cerca de un océano desconocido,
donde los veranos son muy calurosos,
y los habitantes viven en altas montañas
al lado del mar.
Algunos escritores chinos describen a los habitantes
de esta isla como seres con mandíbulas largas,
narices como picos de pájaro, ojos rojos, cabezas blancas
cubiertas con pelo y plumas, capaces de volar
pero no a largas distancias.
Muchos se arriesgan a lanzarse a lo desconocido,
pero la isla siempre se burla de ellos,
y a los que tratan de volar muy alto
los transforma en basura podrida.
Pocos son los que por puro milagro
cuando tratan de ascender al cielo
son transformados en inmortales,
llamados los "huéspedes de plumas"
expresión china que significa
monje taoista.

IV.

No puedo seguir con los cuentos chinos,
porque el emperador me podría mandar a matar.

Four Chinese Stories

I. Metal mirror

An ancient Chinese story
tells of a certain emperor, Ts'in Shi (259-219 B.C.)
who possessed "the precious mirror that will illuminate the bones of the body."
Also known as "the mirror that illuminates the bile."
The mirror appears described as follows:
a rectangle four feet wide by five feet nine inches high,
both its interior and its exterior gleaming.
By putting his hand over his heart, anyone
could see his viscera in the mirror.
When a man stood in front of it to see his reflection,
his image would appear fragmented into tiny circles.
According to another legend, it was a wooden board
from a tree called "the king of chemists."

II. Kites like birds

In a commentary in the *Annals of the Bamboo Books*
the Chinese emperor Shu is described as a "flying being,"
"the first man to descend safe and sound in a parachute,"
and "the one who flew like a bird."
I climb the tower and cannot descend;
my father has set it on fire and everything is collapsing.
It was the 12th century.
Thanks to my good head and my two straw hats,
that provide useful shade in any situation,
I leap off and land on the earth, with my linen tunic spotless.
Definitively, despite my brothers' conspiracies,
centuries later Leonardo da Vinci left me sketched
in one of his many aviation notebooks.
Later the Venetian Fausto Veranzio—perhaps in the 16th century?—

made a number of impulsive brush strokes and modified the design.
I should state that no true descent by parachute
occurred until 1783 in Montpellier.
My knowledge of geography is slight,
and foreign names make my head swim, but even so,
I should acknowledge that history books
sometimes contain some truths,
and besides, I was there. Spotless.

III. Yü min or those who fly

Some Chinese writers tell of a country of flying beings,
an island near an unknown ocean,
where summers are very hot,
and the inhabitants live in high mountains
beside the sea.
Some Chinese writers describe the inhabitants
of this island as beings with large jaws,
noses like bird beaks, red eyes, white heads
covered with hair and feathers, capable of flying
but not for long distances.
Many dare to hurl themselves into the unknown,
but the island always mocks them,
and those who try to fly high up
are transformed into rotten garbage.
Few are those who by pure miracle,
upon attempting to ascend into the sky
are transformed into immortals
called the "feathered guests,"
a Chinese expression that means
Taoist monk.

IV.

I cannot continue with the Chinese stories
because the Emperor might order me killed.

Para Sabina, In Memoriam

Más allá del párpado
se alimenta el ojo
en su inevitable recorrido
hacia lo que a mí me interesa
porque es lo que no soy.

Si hay espacio por recorrer
es aquél que va del cénit
al nadir para encontrarse
en un núcleo.

Después de la primera mirada
no hay quien detenga
el rayo de la pupila,
y si hay dilatación
es porque el vacío
lo ha convertido todo,
lo ha vuelto mosaico,
grano, semilla, y tal vez fruta.

La bondad de la niña del ojo
es clara de huevo,
suspiro agradecido
y toque dulzón entre
varios prismas.

No se trata aquí de ningún sonido,
o quizás sí,
del sonido mudo
de las partículas en la distancia.

Me detengo.
El ojo se detiene y

contempla sin apuro:

la calma del espejo
nace de los amores del
yo consigo mismo.

For Sabina, In Memoriam

Beyond the eyelid
the eye is nourished
by its inevitable shift
toward what interests me
because it is what I am not.

If there is a space to explore
it's the one that spans from zenith
to nadir to find itself
in a nucleus.

After the first look
no one can stop
the pupil's ray,
and if there is dilation
it is because the void
has converted everything,
has turned it all into mosaic,
grain, seed, and perhaps fruit.

The kindness of the apple's eye
is egg white,
grateful sigh
and sweet clink of
several prisms.

It's not a matter here of any sound,
or perhaps it is,
of the mute sound
of particles in a distance.

I pause.
The eye pauses and

contemplates unhurriedly:

the mirror's calm
is born of
self love.

La Poésie est comme lui

Dicen que F. Picabia era cubano, y si es cierto (lo era su padre) celebro su ingenio que no tiene nacionalidad, y su aparición de fantasma por todas partes. Varias frases suyas son casi sus mejores cuadros. Además, me gusta el descapotable que Francis conducía, y su aspecto de tigre. Alta velocidad. Sonrisa en la cámara.

La Poésie est comme lui

They say that F. Picabia was Cuban, and if it is true (his father was) I celebrate his ingenuity that has no nationality and his ghostly appearances all over the place. Several of his sayings are almost his best paintings. Besides, I like the convertible Francis used to drive, and his tiger look. High speed. Smiling at the camera.

Raimundus Lullus se pasea de la mano de Heather Davis por los jardines del archiduque Luis Salvador

Sin lugar a dudas mi querida pelirroja es afortunada. Una mañana en Mallorca ha valido más que cualquier consagración familiar. Y debo agradecerte varias enseñanzas del ojo frente al mar todopoderoso y demasiado intenso del Mediterráneo.

Cuentan los expertos que después de visitar estos jardines junto a los arrecifes, muchos viajeros se dedican a explorar su alma como si jugaran al ajedrez con un contrincante infatigable.

Raimundus Lullus Goes Walking Hand in Hand With Heather Davis Through the Gardens of Archduke Luis Salvador

There's no doubt about it, my beloved redhead is lucky. A morning in Mallorca has been more useful than any family consecration. And I should thank you for showing me how to discover the essence of things beside the all powerful and too intense Mediterranean Sea.

Experts say that after visiting these gardens by the coral, many travelers dedicate themselves to exploring their souls as if they were playing chess with a tireless opponent.

Bitácora

El centro sagrado del universo es una taberna
en el Mediterráneo, para más detalle geográfico,
en Mahón, Menorca.
Allí todos somos pescadores y cartógrafos.
Nuestras cabezas y pies indican el este y el oeste,
y cuando extendemos los brazos aparecen el norte y el sur.
El papel tangible es el aire
y las habaneras a varias voces trazan las rutas y su cruce,
origen de la mítica fundación de muchas ciudades,
de los remolinos de agua inmensa y de las pulsaciones,
huracán inmóvil que hace temblar los paisajes.

Es Cau, Cala Corb.

Binnacle

The sacred center of the universe is a tavern
in the Mediterranean, to be more geographically specific
in Mahón, Menorca.
There we're all fishermen and cartographers.
Our heads and feet point to the east and to the west,
and when we extend our arms, the north and south appear.
The tangible paper is the air
and the many voices of the Habaneras trace out their routes and their crossing,
origin of the mythic foundation of many cities,
of the immense sea eddies and the pulsing,
immobile hurricane that makes landscapes tremble.

It is Cau, Cala Corb.

After Virgilius Bononiensis,
(vista de pájaro de la ciudad de Amberes en 1565)

El cuello a medio cercenar y un movimiento del cuerpo,
trascendiendo el vestido.

After Virgilius Bononiensis,
(A Bird's Eye View of the City of Antwerp in 1565)

Neck half severed and body rippling,
transcending the dress.

Plantin-Moretus

Para David

Un laberinto de pasillos y pequeños salones,
suburbios de cajas de cristal.
Todo se puede imprimir, todo debe ser representado,
todo tiene una forma, y hasta mi ingenua traducción
del italiano, sólo en tu oído, tiene la lectura rigurosa
que hace el linotipista de sus letras de plomo.
¿Te acuerdas de nuestra ciudad maqueta sometida a
la tortura de una luz cruel?
"De muy niño, en Wrexham, donde he nacido,
mi padre solía llevarme de paseo a tocar
los deyectos de la vieja ciudad".
Suprema la línea del Quattrocento y las otras invenciones
de tirar la piedra, andar tras ella, inscribirnos en ella
como actores y encontrar la salida.

Plantin-Moretus

For David

A labyrinth of hallways and little parlors,
suburbs of crystal boxes.
Everything can be printed, everything should be represented,
everything has a shape, and even my ingenuous translation
from the Italian, for your ears only, has the strict reading
the linotypist uses with his lead letters.
Do you remember our city model subjected to
the torture of a cruel light?
"When I was a young boy, in Wrexham, where I was born,
my father used to take me out to touch
the ruins of the old city."
Supreme the line of the Quattrocento and the other inventions
of throwing a stone, going after it, incribing ourselves on it
as actors and finding the exit.

Les cages sont toujours imaginaires

A Max Ernst

No hace tanto tiempo
fui hija de un extraño país,
habité muros de cicatrices
mientras aprendía que nunca
tendría un idioma verdadero.

Han pasado más de veinte años
desde que abandoné mi ciudad:
ella regresa borrosa, en harapos
las más de las veces, otras casi
majestuosa y de anatomía bíblica.

Hay ciudades cuyos sonidos
entran en el oído interno y lo
destrozan, producen una locura
de principiante que bien mirada
se asemeja al patio central de una
vieja casa romana.

Viajeros de paso me cuentan
que las calles de mi antiguo barrio
tienen la forma de un callejón de artesano,
con un tímpano en harapos que honra su percusión,
golpecito y pálpito del desorientado.

Y es así como todo se sabe por allá,
gracias a las ondas sonoras que hacen viajar
vibraciones hasta el pabellón central.

Si se construye algún puente, es movible.
Lo único cierto son laberintos de huesos,

pasajes de fibras y canales hacia cavernas
donde toda narración queda interrumpida
por un quizás.

Ellos son los oyentes por excelencia.

Les cages sont toujours imaginaires

To Max Ernst

Not so long ago
I was the daughter of a strange country,
I inhabited walls of scars
while I learned that I would never
have a true language.

More than twenty years have gone by
since I left my city
now a hazy image, mostly coming back to me
in tatters, but at other times
majestic and possessing Biblical anatomy.

There are cities whose sounds
enter the internal ear and
destroy it, produce a beginner's
madness that, closely considered,
is very much like the central patio
of an old Roman house.

Visitors passing by tell me
that the streets of my old neighborhood
have the shape of a craftsmen's alley,
with a ragged eardrum that honors its percussion,
the light touch and tap of the disoriented.

And that's how people find out about everything there,
thanks to the soundwaves that set off vibrations
in the direction of the central pavilion.

If some bridge is built, it is movable.
The only certainties are the labyrinths of bones,

passages of fibers and canals into caverns
where all narration is always interrupted
by a perhaps.

They are the ideal listeners.

Movimientos metálicos para juguetes abandonados

I

Andrej Ivashnev y Marcella Soltan proyectan una fluidez
siniestra de coyunturas dislocadas y de huesos rotos.
Quiero cantar sobre muñecos gigantescos,
payasos, princesas y monstruos en una procesión
de generaciones y generaciones de gestos macabros.
Conozco a mucha gente que escapa de las pesadillas
con un simple movimiento de cabeza.

II

Un teatro de marionetas convertido en urbe,
contra toda tiranía la memoria recuerda "amenazadora"
y respira "sin mensajes". Se abre el telón y las sombras
se mueven en trance dentro de una catedral invisible
de música industrial.

III

Devastador dominio de un ritual ruso antiguo, movimientos
de goma, y sobre todo difusa danza de la oscuridad.
Cualquier ciudad tiene un río, como Londres lo tiene,
y aquellos que no quieren saber nada abandonan el teatro
espantados, y después compran un pasaje para irse muy lejos,
a algún rincón del mundo donde nadie sepa cuáles son los juguetes
de Bertrand.

Metallic Movements for Abandoned Toys

I

Andrej Ivashnev and Marcella Soltan project a sinister
fluidity of dislocated joints and broken bones.
I want to sing about gigantic dolls,
clowns, princesses and monsters in a procession
of generations and generations of macabre gestures.
I know many people who escape nightmares
with a simple movement of the head.

II

A puppet theater converted into a city,
resistant to all tyranny memory recalls "menacing"
and exhales "without messages." The curtain opens
and the shadows move in a trance within an invisible cathedral
of industrial music.

III

Devastating dominance of an ancient Russian ritual, movements
of rubber, and above all diffuse dance of darkness.
Most cities have rivers, as London has,
and those who don't wish to know anything rush out of the theater
horrified, and later buy a ticket to go somewhere far away,
to some corner of the world where no one knows anything
about Bertrand's toys.

El Libro de Giulio Camillo
(Maqueta para un teatro de la memoria)
The Book of Giulio Camillo
(A Model for a Theater of Memory)

I
ESCRIBO EN AGUA RÁPIDA
el banquete de la mudez: agua
pruebo los sabores de la visión: memoria

II
MEMORIA SÓLO FUE TU BOCA
y la lengua dispersó su fuerza contra el muro,
corrió por su mandato, se humilló ante su trono

III
DESPUÉS EL AGUA SE HIZO REDENTORA
se esculpió en pilares frescos,
esperando más prudencia, menos terror

IV
LA MEMORIA TAMBIÉN ES BUENA
cuando se derrama,
cuando se alza sin súplicas

V
Y LEYERON MI MEMORIA SALIDA DE LOS HUESOS
y la quemaron para adivinar
como herida sagrada en sagrado vaso

VI
FUE CORTA LA MEMORIA
y el recuerdo del recuerdo mismo
dejó que la mano retuviera la palabra

VII
NO SÉ SI PUDE TOCARLA
tejido o textura,
tela urdida con nombres de ciudades

I

IN SWIFT FLOWING WATER I WRITE
the banquet of silence: water
I taste the flavors of vision: memory

II

YOUR MOUTH WAS ONLY MEMORY
and your tongue dispersed its energy against the wall,
it raced at your bidding, it humbled itself before your throne

III

LATER THE WATER BECAME REDEMPTIVE
it sculpted itself into newly made pillars
waiting for more prudence, less terror

IV

MEMORY IS ALSO GOOD
when it overflows
when it rises up without supplication

V

AND THEY READ MY MEMORY DRAWN FROM MY BONES
and they burned it to divine
like a sacred wound in a sacred vessel

VI

MEMORY WAS BRIEF
and the memory of the memory itself
allowed the hand to retain the word

VII

I DON'T KNOW WHETHER I TOUCHED IT
interlaced threads or texture
cloth woven with names of cities

I
MEMORIA CONVERTIDA EN MENSAJERA DE ALIENTOS
de memoria hecha saliva en muchas bocas,
de memoria vuelta multitud de ojos

II
OJO VISUAL ES EL OJO DE LA MENTE
detrás del escenario
la materia prima se mezcla

III
PARA ALZAR LOS SIETE PILARES
que la memoria le pide a la sabiduría,
la reminiscencia es simple mirada

IV
MEMORIA Y MANO ABRAZADAS
bajo el umbral del agua
y el vuelo del pájaro

V
PRESAGIO QUE SE AFANA AL VUELO
de una mudez que oye
el hálito del aire

VI
SIBILANTE COMO EL FUEGO LA PIEL
se acopla con un heliotropo
que está a la mira del cielo

VII
ASIR Y RETENER SON DOS PODERES
de la estancia: memoria
de la travesía: mano

I
MEMORY CONVERTED INTO MESSENGER OF BREATHS
of memory turned to saliva in many mouths,
of memory become a multitude of eyes

II
VISUAL EYE IS THE MIND'S EYE
backstage
prime matter is mixed

III
IN ORDER TO RAISE THE SEVEN PILLARS
that memory asks of wisdom,
reminiscence is simple gaze

IV
MEMORY AND HAND EMBRACING
beneath the water's threshold
and the bird's flight

V
PREMONITION THAT YEARNS FOR FLIGHT
from a silence that hears
the sigh of air

VI
WHISTLING LIKE FIRE, SKIN
couples with a heliotrope
under the sky's gaze

VII
TO GRASP AND TO RETAIN ARE TWO POWERS
of being: memory
of crossing: hand

I

LA MEMORIA SE DISPONE A EMPRENDER VUELO
y hace livianas sus cicatrices, apaga su olor,
a cada cual su piel de hilachas

II

DE IDÉNTICOS HILOS ES MI TRAJE HISTÓRICO
que agradece la zozobra en la piel,
su sueño de sandalias aladas

III

LA MEMORIA SE DESPIERTA EN PAPEL TIMBRADO
con matasellos vagabundo y letra de pluma fina,
despojo de toda visión interior, puro tacto

IV

ALLÍ, SIGNIFICA LA CIUDAD DE LOS ANFITEATROS
aquí, significa la ciudad de los itinerarios,
mi allí y mi aquí se validan: destino

V

LA TOTALIDAD Y EL VACÍO
y las criaturas vivientes
corrieron y volvieron

VI

INFINITO HILO DE SALIVA QUE REGRESA
a imprimir en la memoria
el ojo absoluto de lo súbito

VII

COMO SEMILLA SAGRADA LA MANO PALPA
una niñez urbana de madrugadas estrellas
y palabras de tibias espesuras

I
MEMORY PREPARES TO TAKE FLIGHT
and shrinks its scars, damps its odor
to each his own seamy side

II
MY HISTORIC OUTFIT IS MADE OF IDENTICAL THREADS
it appreciates the skin's anxiety
its dream of winged sandals

III
MEMORY AWAKES ON OFFICIAL PAPER
stamped with errant seals and elegant lettering,
vestige of all inner vision, pure touch

IV
THERE: MEANS THE CITY OF AMPHITHEATRES
here: means the city of itineraries,
my here and my there validate each other: destiny

V
TOTALITY AND VOID
and the living creatures
ran and returned

VI
INFINITE THREAD OF SALIVA THAT COMES BACK
to impress upon memory
the absolute eye of the abrupt

VII
LIKE A SACRED SEED THE HAND FEELS
an urban childhood of dawn stars
and words of warm densities

Quincunce
Quincunx

Por la viva inquietud de la ciudad

Para Isidoro Mauleón, mi maestro.

c.1430-1479 "San Jerónimo en su estudio"

Antonello Da Messina
decide que su capucha blanca
es casi una casa y, sin embargo,
no del todo, no del todo una casa.
Por eso deja que su cartucho de tintas
haga muecas y salpique
la noche, gran papel ácido
(cinto oscuro, isla amarga).

Viaja la mano sabia por tentativas de leyes
con un algo tembloroso
para palpar al final del cuadro
a ese malabarista, tú, que haces muecas,
mientras deslizo mi mano sobre la madera limpia
para que nuestra morada crezca
y se expanda hasta el corazón
de la propia madera (húmeda y rugosa).

Antonello Da Messina
canta hasta que la última gota
y la última migaja desaparezcan.
Canta para que el azar
pida un nuevo plazo.
Canta para que el azar
deje de aturdirse.
Canta para que el azar
tenga pulso bajo su lengua.

Debajo de tu capucha blanca
hay bordes de luz, Antonello.
Esta es la hora que amas: pienso.

Esta hora, la que no pertenece
ni a la tarde ni a la noche.

Canto contigo para que el azar
se quiebre como un cristal,
y deje tu lengua intacta.

Sí, a veces no sólo me olvido
de quién soy, sino de qué soy,
me olvido de ser. — Samuel Beckett, *Molloy*
Y nuestra sonrisa
también se quiebra
en el tejido que cubre tu cabeza.

Llega la noche sobria, y libre de cuidados — Marcial, *Libro 10,* Epigrama 47
con trato fácil y comida sencilla
hacemos que la fe sea una gran sábana blanca
que cubre la ciudad de trapo.

Roma con sus baños, agua siempre agua
y el cielo de Milán como pulpa de fuego.

¿Cómo voy a reconstruir el libro de la memoria?
pregunta Próspero, nuestro huésped, — Peter Greenaway, *Prospero's Book*
mientras contempla cómo su imaginación
se forma y se destruye a sí misma
en la búsqueda del libro total.

Caos pertinaz.
Anulación de las páginas interiores
agua miserable si no es canto
trazado de tiranías que estremece los gestos.

Una escritura de agua ansiosa — Edmond Jabés, *La memoria y la mano*
con círculos concéntricos

agua que late sin transparencia
en mi mano.

Un malabarista hace gestos al final de la calle
y cuando me acerco a verlo
aparece quieto en la vidriera de una librería de uso.
En la plaza romana hay disfraces sueltos
que no tienen preferencias por jóvenes ni viejos.

Antonello, en el tatuaje de mi espalda
llevo las adivinanzas que el dictador prohibiera.

Próspero pide el sonido absoluto del agua
y un papel ácido para dibujar figuras.
La historia del libro es la historia de mi piel,
una historia llena de marcas de agua.

¿Quién gana el juego? se atreve a preguntar el bufón
mientras trazo con pinceladas largas
los perfiles de los dos maestros.

Ahora los colores se confunden:
es la hora que amo, piensa,
es la hora del mirlo y de la lechuza que se acerca, dice,
es la hora de la luz dorada de los eucaliptos, escribe.

(Yo me paseo con el maestro y su perro)

El bufón ha decidido que no hay que anhelar el día postrero.

Agua cae sobre agua.

Cenamos hoy a puerta cerrada, Marcial dulcísimo,
pero primero deja que tus oídos

salgan a la calle, quizás Fortuna llame
y nos ofrezca otra silla.

La noche llega, y una tormenta lanza la mano
a velocidad sorprendente,
la mano versada en aguas
identifica el papel.
Suma de todos los colores en la oscuridad:
San Jerónimo en su estudio
prolonga la sed de Próspero.
Llega el agua de la memoria.
Voces. Voces.

Libro de agua

Oscuridad que dulcifica la circulación de la sangre
mi sangre es ya lo suficientemente circular
lo suficientemente mezclada:
un no-color, una transparencia
que entra con lentitud de nada.

Jack Foley, "Sweeney Adrift"

Suibne de Ros Earcain es mi nombre,
soy el loco, el demente,
déjenme entrar.
Cuando la noche llega no descanso
y no pisan mis pies trillada senda.
Aquí no habitaré largo tiempo: los lazos
del miedo ya me ciñen.

De *"Suibne, el loco"*, anónimo irlandés, Siglo XII

Risas y voces. La tempestad pasa las páginas:

Próspero lee en voz alta:

He aquí, Marcial dulcísimo, lo que alegra la vida:
una hacienda heredada, no la hecha con esfuerzo:
un campo agradecido, un hogar siempre ardiente;

usar poco la toga, no tener nunca un pleito;
tranquilidad de espíritu, robustez natural,
prudente sencillez, amigos de igual genio,
trato fácil, comida sencilla, noche sobria
y libre de cuidados; alegre y puro lecho,
sueño que haga las sombras breves; desear ser
lo que eres, sin tener preferencia por eso
o aquello: finalmente, no tener miedo alguno,
ni tampoco anhelar, el día postrimero.

Marcial, *Libro 10,* Epigrama 47

Sopla el viento.

Libro de espejos

Otra historia yo sé, dice Suibne, y es ya famosa:
me entristece contarla, murmura Próspero.

Hojas de mercurio. Hojas de plata.
Antonello pasa las páginas.

Mano con dedos sin aliento,
vino que me alcanza,
herido estoy de hambre, siendo un loco.

Algunas páginas reflejan al lector
mientras intenta leer
traslúcido papel.
Otras páginas reflejan al lector
en viaje hacia su memoria niña.
Tal es el bebedizo de las lecciones de papel.
Libros. Sólo libros.

Mano que reconoce.
Mano ala que sabe de árboles interiores.

Yo paso, más veloz que las alondras;
en carrera grandiosa y rauda, me persiguen,

y salto por encima de los caídos troncos
al traspasar las cimas.

Cuando, orgullosa, huye
de nosotros la tórtola,
no tardo en alcanzarla,
pues me han nacido plumas.

-Por el amor de Dios—dice Próspero—,
déjame brincar mi locura trasterrada.
Tú, errabundo, escaso de vestido;
yo me vigilo a mí mismo
en el parloteo de la tormenta,
raposillas que ladran
rauda carrera de la tormenta que imagino.

Intento el inventario de mis libros,
quiero alzarme contra ésta, mi sed viva
en los rostros de mis enemigos
contra los que ahora bramo.
Otra historia yo sé, dejen hablar a Suibne, el loco.

Pinto un escenario que se destruye a sí mismo,
más me place oír al tejón, Antonello.

Agua que bala, gota pequeñísima
que sacude mil veces el tatuaje de mi espalda.

Epílogo

Hay un poema que se está formando antes de que la mano
se abra enorme y traspase estos harapos.

Through the Alert Restlessness of the City

For Isidoro Mauleón, mi maestro.

c. 1430-1479 "St Jerome in his study"

Antonello Da Messina
decides that his white hood
is almost a house, and yet still,
not quite, not quite a house.
that's why he allows his inky cartridge
to make faces and splash
the night, a great acid paper
(dark belt, bitter island).

The wise hand travels through attempted laws
with a bit of shakiness
to touch at the painting's end
that juggler, you, who are making faces,
while I run my hand over the clean wood
so that our dwelling may grow
and expand to the very heart
of the wood itself (humid and rough).

Antonello Da Messina
sings until the last drop
and the last crumb have vanished.
He sings so that chance
may ask for a new turn.
He sings so that chance
may recover itself.
He sings so that chance
can revive the pulse beneath its tongue.

Under your white hood
there are fringes of light, Antonello.
This is the hour you love, I think.

This hour, the one that belongs
neither to the afternoon nor to the night.

I sing with you so that chance
will shatter like a pane of glass,
and leave your tongue intact.

Yes, sometimes I not only forget
who I am, but what I am,
I forget to be.
And our smile — Samuel Beckett, *Molloy*
also shatters
in the woven cloth that covers your head.

The sober night falls, and free of cares — Martial, *Book 10,* Epigram 47
with pleasant manner and simple food
we turn faith into a big white sheet
that covers the rag city.

Rome with its baths, water ever water
and the city of Milan like fiery pulp.

"How am I going to reconstruct the book of
memory?," asks Prospero, our host, — Peter Greenaway, *Prospero's Book*
while he contemplates how his imagination
creates and destroys itself
in the search for the total book.

Persistent chaos.
Destruction of the inner pages
miserable water if it is not song a blueprint
of tyrannies, making gestures shudder.

A writing of anxious water — Edmond Jabés, *Memory and The Hand*
with concentric circles:

water that pulsates without transparency
in my hand.

A juggler gestures at the end of the street
and when I go over to see him
he appears, still, in the window of a second hand bookstore.
In the Roman plaza there are scattered costumes
that favor neither the young nor the old.

Antonello, the tattoo on my back shows
the riddles that the dictator prohibited.

Prospero requests the absolute sound of the water
and an acid paper on which to draw figures.
The history of the book is the history of my skin,
a history filled with watermarks.

Who wins the game? The jester dares to ask
while with long strokes I sketch
the profiles of the two maestros.

Now the colors blur together:
it's the hour I love, he thinks,
it's the hour of the blackbird and the approaching owl, he says,
it's the hour of the eucalyptus in golden light, he writes.

(I go for a walk with the maestro and his dog)

The jester has decided that we needn't yearn for the last day

Water falls on water.

We dine today behind a closed door, sweet Martial,
but first allow your ears

to go out on the street, Fortune may call
and offer us another chair.

Night falls, and a storm throws out the hand
with astonishing rapidity,
the hand expert in waters
identifies the paper.
A blend of all colors in the darkness:
St. Jerome in his studio
prolongs Prospero's thirst.
The water of memory arrives.
Voices. Voices.

Book of Water

Darkness that sweetens the blood's circulation
by now my blood is sufficiently circular
sufficiently mixed:
a non-color, a transparency
that enters with the gradualness of nothing.

Jack Foley, "Sweeny Adrift"

Suibne of Ros Earcain is my name,
I am the madman, the demented one,
let me enter.
When night falls I do not rest
and my feet do not tread the usual path.
I will not live here for long: the bonds
of fear are already tightening around me.

From *Suibne the Madman,* anonymous Irish writer, 12th c.

Laughter and voices. The storm turns the pages:

Prospero reads out loud:

Here we have, dear Martial, what makes life joyful:
an inherited estate, not one established with effort:
grateful lands, an ever blazing hearth,
seldom a need to don the toga, never an argument;

a peaceful spirit, natural good health,
prudent simplicity, good natured friends,
conviviality, simple food, early Martial, *Book 10*, Epigram 47
carefree nights; a happy and pure bed,
sleep that makes the nighttime hours short; glad to be
who you are, without craving this or that:
finally, to be free of any fear,
or any yearning for the final day. *Book of Mirrors*

The wind blows.

I know another story, says Suibne, and it's already famous.
It makes me sad to tell it, whispers Prospero.

Leaves of mercury. Leaves of silver.
Antonello turns the pages.

A hand with lifeless fingers,
intoxicated by wine,
I'm wounded by hunger, being a madman.

Some pages reflect the reader
while he tries to read
translucent paper.
Other pages reflect the reader
traveling toward childhood memory.

Such is the potion of the paper lessons.
Books. Only books.

A hand that recognizes.
Wing hand wise in interior trees.

I race past, swifter than the larks
in a tremendous rush, they pursue me,

and I jump over the fallen tree trunks
as I run through the treetops.

When the turtledove flees
from us proudly,
I catch up to it quickly
for I've sprouted feathers.

"For the love of God," says Prospero,
"Let me forget my exiled madness."
You, wanderer, half undressed;
I'll look after myself
in the chatter of the storm
vixen barking
swift race of the storm I imagine.

I attempt an inventory of my books,
I want to rise against it, my active thirst
in the face of my enemies
I bellow out against them.
I know another story: let Suibne the madman speak.

I paint a scenario that self-destructs,
I prefer to hear the badger, Antonello.

Water that beats, tiny drop
that shakes the tattoo on my back a thousand times.

Epilogue

There is a poem forming before the hand can
open wide and pierce these rags.

Oquedad del caracol (soplo divino)

Dedicado al poeta hebreo Yair Hurvitz (1941-1988).

Y han de decir: "Un poco de humo
se retorcía en cada gota de su sangre."

Gilberto Owen

Poseo, al parecer, inclinación religiosa;
una prueba: una lengua suficiente
a contener, directa, fina y sólida
me ha llevado a los cinco rumbos
del universo: *Quincunce.*

Patio de cuatro habitaciones
que inclina sus múltiples formas,
que reside en la materia
que tiene envolturas vitales:
pasillos ceremoniales
de otras arquitecturas.

Lo mismo que la chispa divina engendra en la tierra
toda su riqueza, así el *Quincunce,* semilla
de una cosmología revelada, florece en un deslumbrante
sistema de imágenes y diseños arquitectónicos que,
por pertenecer al universo de las formas, padece
frecuentemente de una lógica elemental engañadora.

Guillermo Marín, *Mitla, ciudad de los muertos*

Lo que completa este texto
son monumentales piedras
allí donde una mano supo
mover, tallar y ensamblar.

La voz de Eduardo traza un mapa de México en la tierra
mientras narra que "los cronistas de la colonia nunca
se refirieron a la arquitectura de Mitla sin una mezcla de aversión
y admiración... Para hablar entonces de Mictlán (lugar de los muertos),
tenemos que desprendernos de la concepción occidental de la muerte..."

Mi mareo absurdo ya no se mece en las ramas del árbol del tule;
ahora, en tierra de espíritus, se contenta con un soplo del viento
y una risotada audaz que perfora mis tímpanos. Sí, las campanas
de la iglesia han empezado a liberar un esplendor vigente y murmullos:
Piénsese así, que entre los escombros de mi energía se eleva de pronto
una presencia, semejante a un recinto, puerta de alusiones musicales.

Me separo del grupo.
Me contento con ver.
Importa. Varias campanadas de aire
se curvan sobre mi
audacia que no me falta
y ciudad de voces
allí donde el viento
no es cosa ajena al oído
ni ver a los espíritus
un acto de sombras interiores.

Lo que podía amar se borra,
y ojos y labios, luz y humedad,
quedan deshilachados.
El enigma de sabores
también queda resuelto.
La noche anterior los besos
cruzaron dos puntos lingüísticos.
Ahora no hay diálogo.

De los cuatro puntos cardinales
se levantará en pocos momentos una fría y
poco generosa ráfaga de viento. Te disolverás.

Mi muerte está asociada con la tierra,
pero el otro muerto en cuestión
tendrá que pasar un largo y caudaloso río.

Techichi el perrito lo guiará:
sin vestiduras pasará cerros erizados
y beberá tormentas terribles.
El viento le cortará la piel
como naranja.

Más que toda desgarradura, peor que la propia muerte,
"Lo que daña es tocar el cuerpo, darse largos
besos y unir el muslo con el muslo".

Albio Tibulo, *Libro I , Poema VIII*

Con visión transfigurada,
Fray Bernardo de Alburquerque,
mandó construir entre 1535 y 1580
la fachada del costado norte
de la catedral de Oaxaca a semejanza...

Del patio de cuatro habitaciones se extienden grecas móviles
de agua. Leo: ni sacrificios de armadillos, conejos, pájaros y
venados lograban satisfacer la ira de los dioses contra los
poco generosos de espíritu. A los tacaños se les condenaba
a un palacio subterráneo a izar oscuridades.

Otra vez la voz de Eduardo se confunde con mi torrente mental
que circunda a las portentosas montañas, copula con la piedra
y bebe las gotas de leche del árbol que alimentaba a los niños muertos.
Habitantes de las nubes. Ramas de las que me cuelgo.
Lieder de Schumann que se confunde con mis propias visiones.

Lenguas copiosas de la piedra: escuchar, reconocer,
descender al interior de una jacaranda:
formular el patio interior
"fue volver a la pista de mi verso
después de morderme mucho las manos sin motivo
y de patalear con duda e ira".

Propercio, *Libro I*, *Poema IV*

Unos dísticos elegíacos me azotan con demasiada destreza.
¿Qué hago yo en el centro de la ciudad de los muertos
tarareando mil tonadillas y con todos aquellos poemas
rompiéndoseme encima?

¿Qué hace mi piel convertida en esponjosa sustancia,
disfrutando de cada marca de voces y trazos,
cada perforación, cada gota de sangre de mis poros?

Bendita rememoración,
allí donde una mueca desdeñosa
me ofrece paisajes.
Bendita desdicha de bordes rotos
que hace al corazón medio profeta,
ese "das harts iz a halber novi"
que se completa y se escucha
en un sistema de imágenes:
azota y voltea con destreza,
pues nací en una ciudad con mar
desde arenas demasiado blancas,
y nunca hice pacto
con sus aires calientes
ni sus sales proyectadas en mis sombras.
Si la brisa marina me quitó la respiración,
me ahogué y fui resucitada. Y mi madre,
que no podía escuchar las voces que rondaban
por toda la casa y que iban conmigo,
habló a solas con la nana Blasa.

Después me pusieron un amuleto sobre el pecho,
allí donde nadie podía ver presencias ni memorias.
Sólo pienso en toda la audacia que me ha faltado
para volver a escuchar las voces,
ahora levantadas, extremas, sin recato de mudez,
batalla florida de mi propia alma.

Inner Chamber of the Seashell (Divine Whisper)

Dedicated to the Hebrew poet Yair Hurvitz (1941-1988)

And they will say: "A bit of smoke
writhed in each drop of his blood. "

Gilberto Owen

It would seem that I possess a religious bent;
a proof: a tongue sufficient
to contain, direct, refined, and solid
has led me to the five points
of the universe: *Quincunx.*

Four-room courtyard
that inclines its multiple forms
that resides in matter
that has vital layers
ceremonial passageways
of other architectures.

Just as the divine spark engenders in the earth
life in all its richness, thus the *Quincunx*, seed
of a revealed cosmology, flowers in a dazzling
system of images and architectural designs that,
by being part of the universe of forms, suffers
frequently from a deceptively elemental logic.

Guillermo Marín,
Mitla, City of the Dead

What completes this text
are monumental stones
there where a hand learned how
to move, sculpt and assemble.

Eduardo's voice traces a map of Mexico on the earth
while he tells of how "the colonial chroniclers never
referred to the architecture of Mitla without combined aversion
and admiration... Thus to speak of Mictlán (place of the dead)
we must detach ourselves from the Western concept of death..."

My absurd dizziness no longer rocks in the branches of the tule tree;
now, in the land of the spirits, it is content with a puff of wind
and a bold guffaw that perforates my eardrums. Yes, the church bells
have begun to set loose a timely splendor and murmurs:
Think of it this way, that amid the rubble of my energy suddenly looms
a presence, like that of a hallowed place, door of musical allusions.

I detach myself from the group.
I am content to see.
It matters. Several bolts of air
swerve around my
unfailing audacity
and city of voices
there where the wind
does not sound unfamiliar to the ear
nor is seeing spirits
an act of inner shadows.

What could be loved is erased
and eyes and lips, light and humidity
are stripped bare.

The enigma of flavors
is also resolved.
The night before, kisses
crossed two linguistic points.
Now there is no dialogue.

From the four cardinal points

will soon rise a cold and
ungenerous gust of wind. You will dissolve.

My death is associated with the earth,
but the other dead man in question
will have to cross a long and mighty river.

Techichi the little dog will guide him:
naked he will cross spiky peaks
and drink terrible storms.
The wind will slice his skin
like an orange.

More than any heartbreak, worse than death
itself, "What hurts is touching the body,
long kisses, and pressing thigh to thigh."

Albius Tibullus, *Book I, Poem VIII*

With transfigured vision,
Friar Bernardo of Alburquerque
ordered construction of the north façade
of the Oaxaca cathedral
between 1535 and 1580, in the image...

From the four-room courtyard flow moving friezes of water.
I read: the gods' anger with those who are ungenerous in spirit
was not placated by sacrifices of armadillos, rabbits, birds
and deer. Misers were condemned
to a subterranean palace to hoist dark shadows.

Once again Eduardo's voice blends with my mental torrent
that encircles the marvelous mountains, copulates with the stone
and drinks milk droplets from the tree that used to nourish dead children.
Inhabitants of the clouds. Branches from which I hang.
Schumann lieder that fuse with my own visions.
Copious tongues of rock: to listen, to recognize,

to descend to the interior of a jacaranda:
to design the interior patio
"was to get back onto the trail of my poem Propertius, *Book I, Poem IV*
after biting my hands unreasonably
and stamping my feet in doubt and anger."

Some elegiac distiches pound me with excessive skill.
What am I doing in the center of the city of the dead
humming a thousand popular tunes and with all those
poems breaking over me?

What is my skin doing turned into a spongy substance
enjoying each voicemark and stroke,
each perforation, each drop of blood that seeps from my pores?

Blessed recollection,
there where a scornful grimace
offers me landscapes.
Blessed misery of broken borders
that turns the heart into a semi prophet.
that "das harts iz a halber novi"
that is completed and heard
by a system of images:
it hits and turns with skill
for I was born in a city by the sea
with excessively white sands
and I never made a pact
with its hot winds
or its salts projected in my shadows.

If the sea breeze took my breath away,
I drowned and was resuscitated. And my mother
who couldn't hear the voices that filled
the whole house and went with me,
spoke alone with nanny Blasa.

Later they put an amulet on my chest,
there where no one could see presences or memories.
I think only of all the courage I've lacked
to go back to hearing the voices,
raised now, loud, without any semblance of
restraint, flowery battle of my own soul.

En la ansiedad de mi ojo, una súbita cesación del tiempo

Galileo Galilei, con su telescopio del siglo XVII
se pone a mirar la noche. Todo cambia.
Luz. Ojo humano destellante.
Instrumentos ópticos infinitos.
En 1789, William Herschel
se recrea con un telescopio
de cuarenta pies frente a Urano.
John, hijo de Willi (así lo llaman sus amigos),
juega en negativo y positivo
con fotografías curiosas.
Algún tiempo después, Ansel Adams
imagina paisajes sin memoria.

Antes de que Marcel Duchamp
creara su *Étant donnés* en 1943,
un metereólogo principiante,
un tal Luke Howard,
se dedica en el siglo XVIII
a mirar el cielo por los ojos de las cerraduras.

-Veo nubes altas e inmensas que se acumulan
y crean castillos mutables.
-Veo finas colas de yeguas.
-Veo pequeñas gotas de agua,
y en el frío de la altura, cristales de hielo, dice.

Trampa visual en una puerta de Cadaqués.
El telescopio existe para dar forma al ojo,
y hay un rayo de luz que acecha tras la puerta.
Lo hermético es el *vas bene clausum*
para el mirón-voyeur que camina
por un largo pasillo y es puro ojo
y lentas manos para abrir la escena.

Cae el agua y el gas ilumina.
Mise à nu: aguzo el ojo tras una puerta mugrosa
y es una tarde de 1994. Hace calor en Filadelfia
y veo uno de tus ojos: "Ich hörte sagen" (oí decir)
la profecía de las cinco codornices que me soplas dentro del alma.

Para contar mis visiones
de esta noche comencemos
nombrando a Comenius.
Se trata aquí de un peregrino,
también conocido como vagabundo,
caminador y el que pasa.
Se trata aquí de calles y aprendizajes prácticos
en cualquier ciudad del mundo.
Se trata aquí de un escritor del siglo XVII
que se encuentra con algunos astrónomos y astrólogos
en su recorrido por el laberinto del corazón.
Se trata aquí de hombres que conjuran horóscopos
e inventan profecías al observar los cuerpos celestes.
Se trata aquí del señor Ubiquitous
que me guía hasta una terraza.
Se trata aquí de varios astrólogos
lanzando escaleras al cielo,
cazando estrellas y gritando
que el firmamento esta noche
carece de equilibrio, sí,
anomalitas coeli.
Esta noche las estrellas no bailan
a la música de los observadores,
dice el peregrino. Allí está el cometa.

-En mis memorias infantiles
hay estrellas fugaces,
dragones alados y fuegos extraños
en el firmamento, te digo.

Hay ciudades que siembran un poco de locura
en el cerebro de sus habitantes, y todo lo que no ha sido posible
en otros lugares, por extrañas fuerzas ocultas encuentra en ellas terreno propicio.
Hay ciudades que tienen cielos como linternas mágicas.
La Habana, Dublín, Barcelona, Palma de Mallorca, Zürich, Las Cruces,
New Orleans y Praga perforan las pupilas y están habitadas por demonios
siniestros que persiguen a los solitarios.

Rodolfo II se rodea en Praga
de metereólogos y separadores de nubes,
si alguien sabe de quienes se trata.
Voyeurs que como perros cazadores
van detrás de lo que traerá el futuro.
Por eso, Tycho Brahe,
astrólogo de muchos ardides,
puede sobrevivir
con su nariz de hierro y tocar
los techos de las casas enanas
de los alquimistas.

Obligas a tus hombres de pelo largo
(los del Callejón de Oro)
a esperar por mi señal
para las transmutaciones.
Meto el hombro y salgo tatuada.
Destruta, ruinata et devastata
mi espalda da fiero calor,
a quien mucho le plazca,
le dolerá la cabeza.

Cicatriz cuya leña no da el artífice al fuego.
La madreselva es flexible,
y no hay que quemar el esbelto avellano.

Y la que da más fiero calor es la encina,
asegura un anónimo irlandés del siglo XIII.
Y la piel me arde bajo una aguja que crea pura fibra.
Me desintegro en 8' 46", tiempo justo
para que escuches el "Zigeunerweisen" de Sarasate,
interpretado por la orquesta sinfónica de Pittsburgh,
bajo la dirección de André Previn
y con el violín de Itzhak Perlman.

Necesito pequeñas gotas de agua,
o en el frío de la altura, cristales de hielo, digo.

Después hablamos con los *handrlata,*
hombres itinerantes, recogedores de trastos,
de las calles de Praga con sus sacos enormes
sobre los hombros. Maestros en trapos
y en voces chillonas:
"Handrle-handrlevu?" "¿Tiene algo para vender?"
Los viejos de piel arrugada y transparente
como paja se pasean
por la calle Telegraph de Berkeley.
Los seguimos.

El tiempo de la memoria implora sin aliento
que lo salven del envejecimiento,
de ese abismo pegajoso,
que le devuelvan su juventud.
Me miro al espejo y con mano cuarteada
toco el mapa de mis arrugas.
En los últimos cuatro años he envejecido,
me murmuras, mientras de tu boca
sale el alfabeto de mi noche.
Miro por el ojo de una cerradura
y veo cómo tus manos miden
con guita, bramante y compás mi cuerpo.

Lo único que no me gusta de ti es tu pelo.

Las manecillas de nuestro reloj
se mueven hacia atrás.
Un verso de Apollinaire
y otro de Cendrars
son la fórmula para la inmortalidad
de mi cuello.

¿Quién me iba a decir que dormiría por nueve días
en la misma habitación de Kafka en el Graben Hotel de Viena?

Ivan Klima me mira con sus ojillos de cuervo.
Un cielo azul muy claro puede resultar aburrido.

-Quiero un cielo con nubes que se confundan,
con locos que rían y oscuridades de tormenta, dices.

Me desvisto con lentitud asombrosa.
Tras los pasos de mi maestro voy sacando
una a una mis pinturas enrolladas. Te las enseño.
Disfrutamos un rato. Las recojo. Te las vuelvo a enseñar.
Disfrutamos un rato. Hablamos. Toco el número de tu tatuaje.
-Intentaron envenenarme.
Destila el *aurum potabile.*
Pruébala.
Tengo miedo.
Me corta la garganta, dices en sueños.

Quisieras ser como la Elena Marty de Capek
con trescientos años de vida
sin una sola arruga y varias identidades.
¿Acaso no has sido varios yo-tú-ese otro,
escondido, perseguido y torturado?

Eres lo suficientemente bello
como para dejar a cualquiera sin aliento.
Soy también una de tus Elsas.
Pero recuerda Amado mío
que nadie puede desear por 300 años.
Nadie puede tener ilusiones, crear,
observar con ojo eficaz por 300 años.
Es imposible. Uno se cansa de todo.
Me canso.
Y de pronto te das cuenta de que nada existe.
Nada. Ni siquiera la culpa.
Ni siquiera el dolor.
Ni siquiera tú mismo.
Absolutamente nada.

-Sí, tiene buen sabor esta agua mansa,
pero guárdate de ella, dice Comenius.

No hay paraísos del corazón.
Sólo laberintos.
La quintaesencia del universo
se deriva del ojo ameno que mira.

Astrónomos, astrólogos y destiladores
inventan la rajadura del cristal
(agua que no moja las manos).

-Un cuerpo yace sobre la yerba como un animal muerto, me dices.
Cuerpo reflejado en la retina que se desnuda a fuerza de luz secreta.
Estado de desnudez. Descendemos al fondo de la luz (y es el agua).

In the Anxiety of My Eye, Time Suddenly Stops

Galileo Galilei, with his 17th century telescope
begins to gaze at the night. Everything changes.
Light. Gleaming human eye.
Infinite optical instruments.
In 1789, William Herschel
enjoys a forty foot telescope
to behold Uranus.
John, son of Willi (his friends all call him this),
plays in negative and positive
with curious photographs.
A while later, Ansel Adams
imagines landscapes without memory.

Before Marcel Duchamp
created his *Étant donnés* in 1943,
A newfledged meterologist,
one Luke Howard,
devotes himself in the 18th century
to skygazing through keyholes.

"I see tall and immense clouds that accumulate
and create shifting castles."
"I see the delicate tails of mares."
"I see tiny droplets of water,
and in the high altitude cold, ice crystals," he says.

A visual trick on a door in Cadaqués.
The telescope exists to shape the eye,
and there is a ray of light that lurks behind the door.
The hermetic is the *vas bene clausum*
for the unblinking voyeur who walks
down a long passageway and it is pure eye
and slow hands to open the scene.

Water falls and gas illuminates.
Mise à nu: my eye focuses behind a filthy door
and it is an afternoon in 1994. It's a hot day in Philadelphia
and I see one of your eyes: "ich hörte sagen" (I heard you say)
the prophecy of the five quails that you whisper to me within my soul.

To recount my visions
of this evening we begin
by naming Comenius.
I am speaking here of a pilgrim
also known as a vagabond,
a walker and a passer-by.
I am speaking here of streets and practical apprenticeships
in any city of the world.
I am speaking here of a seventeenth century writer
who meets up with some astronomers and astrologists
while on his journey through the heart's labyrinth.
I am speaking here of men who conjure up horoscopes
and invent prophecies as they observe celestial bodies,
I am speaking here of mister Ubiquitous
who guides me to a terrace.
I am speaking here of various astrologers
raising ladders to the sky,
hunting down stars and shouting
that tonight's firmament
lacks equilibrium, yes,
anomalitas coeli.
Tonight the stars do not dance
to the music of observers,
says the pilgrim. The comet is over there.

"In my childhood memories
there are fugitive stars,
winged dragons and strange fires
in the firmament," I tell you.

There are cities that sow a little madness
in the minds of their inhabitants, and all that has not been possible
in other places, through strange occult forces finds propitious terrain there.
There are cities with skies like magic lanterns
Havana, Dublin, Barcelona, Palma de Mallorca, Zürich, Las Cruces,
New Orleans and Prague perforate pupils and are inhabited by sinister
demons that pursue the solitary.

Rudolph II surrounds himself in Prague
with meterologists and cloud splitters,
if anyone knows who those might be.
Voyeurs who, like hunting dogs,
chase after whatever the future will bring.
Thus Tycho Brahe,
astrologer of many ruses,
can survive
with his iron nose and touch
the roofs of the dwarf houses
of the alchemists.

You oblige your long haired men
(the ones from the Golden Alley)
to await my sign
for the transmutations.
I get into danger and come away tatooed.
Destruta, ruinata et devastata
my back gives off blazing heat,
anyone who is very pleased by my fate
will have a headache.

A scar whose kindling is not offered by the inventor to the fire.
The honeysuckle is flexible,
and it's not necessary to burn the slender hazelnut tree.
The one that produces the hotest fire is the oak,

claims an anonymous thirteenth century Irish poem.
And my skin burns under a needle that creates pure fiber.
I disintegrate in 8' 46", the precise duration of the composition
you need to listen to Sarasate's "Zigeunerweisen"
played by the Pittsburgh Symphony Orchestra,
conducted by André Previn
and with Itzhak Perlman as violinist.

"I need tiny droplets of water,
or in the high altitude cold, ice crystals," I say.

Later, we talk to the *handrlata,*
itinerant men, junk collectors,
on the Prague streets, hauling their enormous sacks
on their shoulders. Experts of the rag trade
and of ear piercing cries:
"Handrle-handrlevu?" "Have anything to sell?"
Old folk with wrinkled and transparent skin like straw
stroll along Telegraph Avenue in Berkeley.
We follow them.

The time of memory implores breathlessly
that we save it from aging,
from that sticky abyss,
that we restore its youth.
I gaze at myself in the mirror and with an age-furrowed hand
I touch the map of my wrinkles.
I've aged in the last four years,
you murmur to me, while from your mouth
flows the alphabet of my night.
I look through the keyhole
and I see how your hands measure
my body with string, twine and compass.

The only thing I don't like about you is your hair.

The little hands of our clock
move backwards.
A line of Apollinaire
and another by Cendrars
are the formula for my neck's
immortality.

Who was going to tell me that I'd spend nine days
sleeping in the same room as Kafka in the Graben Hotel in Vienna?

Ivan Klima looks at me with his little crow's eyes.
A very clear blue sky can be boring.

"I want a sky full of intercrossing clouds,
of laughing madmen and a storm darkening," you say.

I undress with astonishing slowness.
Behind my master's footsteps I pull out
my rolled up paintings, one by one. I show them to you.
We relax for a bit. I gather them up. I show them to you again.
We relax for a bit. We chat. I touch your tatooed number.
"They tried to poison me."
The *aurum potabile* drips, distilled.
Drink it.
I'm afraid.
"It cuts my throat," you say in your sleep.

You'd like to be like Capek's Elena Marty,
three hundred years old,
without a single wrinkle and several identities.
Haven't you been various I-You-That Other Ones,
hidden, persecuted and tortured?

You're handsome enough
to leave any woman breathless.

I'm one of your Elsas, too.
But remember, my Beloved,
that no one can desire for three hundred years.
No one can sustain illusions, create,
observe with a sharp eye for three hundred years.
It's impossible. One gets tired of anything.
I'm tired.
And suddenly you realize that nothing exists.
Nothing. Not even blame.
Not even pain.
Not even you yourself.
Absolutely nothing.

"Yes, this spring water tastes good,
but watch out for it," says Comenius.

The heart has no paradises.
Only labyrinths.
The quintessence of the universe
is derived from the gaze of the pleasant eye.

Astronomers, astrologers and destillers
invent the crack in the crystal
(water that doesn't moisten hands).

"A body lies on the grass like a dead animal," you tell me.
A body reflected in the retina that the power of secret light strips bare.
State of nudity. We descend to the bottom of the light (and it is water).

Islario general
Compendium of All the World's Islands

Amach, el maestro Zen y confidente sin par de una poeta llamada Carlota Caulfield

I.

Tuve un gato llamado Amach.
Me besaba cada mañana con su nariz rubia,
y sus abrazos eran ráfagas de ternura exquisita.

Nació en New Orleans y creció en un jardín salvaje.
Viajó conmigo del sur al este y del este al oeste
en maleta de sedas verdes, siempre a mi lado.
Sus tarjetas de embarque llevaban su fotografía
y unas cuantas marcas de colmillos.
Le gustaba saborear papel impreso.

Entre sus manjares estuvieron
la palabra mariposa en cien idiomas
(poema visual de Xavier Canals),
una carta de amor que me escribió
un hombre muy bello,
las páginas de una edición de
poesía irlandesa, algunos pedazos
de los pensamientos de Gracián
y poemas de Michaux. Así era mi gato.
Ávido gourmet que sólo seleccionaba lo mejor:
salmón fresco y pedacitos de hígado,
su última cena, el día antes de morir.

Detestaba un cassette de los poetas de Orígenes
(regalo de Jesús J. Barquet)
que yo trataba de escuchar a veces por la noche.
Aullaba inconsolable ante la voz de Lezama,
y se lanzaba suplicante a mi pecho para que

se hiciera el silencio.
Pero disfrutaba de Jacques Brel, Annie Girardot
y Serge Gainsbourg. Bach y Vivaldi también le gustaban.

2.

Sólo tú supiste, gato amado
de mis alegrías, de mis desasosiegos,
secretos entre nosotros aquellos tantos
bajo tus rubias orejas guerreras
atentas a los sonidos de mis pasos,
siempre y más allá del recibimiento y del juego.
Nuestras confidencias fueron abrazo diario,
beso del amanecer, compañía bendecida
por el misterio de la reencarnación.

Te escribo este poema mientras escucho
un viejo cassette de música de Bach
tan de tu gusto, con las manos de Alex Hug
sobre el teclado del órgano de la Fraumünster,
que conocías bien por mis cuentos, y todas aquellas lágrimas
derramadas frente a los vitrales suizos de Chagall.

Te escribo este poema y mis ojos salen por la ventana
de mi cuarto, tu preferida, y visitan la piedra irlandesa,
morada de tus despojos en este patio de hojas secas
y humedades sin nombre.

Entras y sales a tu voluntad,
cuando en noches de insomnio
eres mi mejor compañero,
tú, mi amigo.

Amach, the Zen Master and Unrivaled Confidant of a Poet Named Carlota Caulfield

I.

I had a cat named Amach.
He kissed me every morning with his yellow nose,
and his embraces brushed me with exquisite tenderness.

Born in New Orleans, he grew up in an overgrown garden.
He traveled with me from south to east and east to west
in a green silk case, always at my side.
His travel documents bore his photograph,
the edges punctured by his fangs.
He liked the taste of printed paper.

Among his favorite treats were
the word butterfly in one hundred languages
(a visual poem by Xavier Canals),
a love letter written to me
by a very handsome man,
the pages of a collection
of Irish poems, some scraps
of Gracián's *Art of Worldly Wisdom*
and poems by Michaux. That's how my cat was.
An avid gourmet who chose only the best:
fresh salmon and tidbits of liver,
his last supper, the day before he died.

He loathed a cassette of the Orígenes poets
(a gift from Jesús J. Barquet)
that I sometimes tried to listen to at night.
Lezama's voice made him howl inconsolably
and he'd hurl himself frantically at my chest,

pleading for silence.
But he enjoyed Jacques Brel, Annie Girardot
and Serge Gainsbourg. He also liked Bach and Vivaldi.

2.

Only you, beloved cat, knew about
my joys and my anxieties,
so many secrets shared only by us,
kept under your warlike golden ears
attentive to the sounds of my footsteps,
ever attuned to rituals of welcome and play.
Our confidences were a daily communion,
a kiss at dawn, companionship blessed
by the mystery of reincarnation.

I write you this poem while I listen
to an old cassette of Bach's music,
just what you liked, with Alex Hug's hands
on the keyboard of the Fraumünster organ,
so familiar to you from my stories, and all those tears
shed before the Swiss Chagall windows.

I write you this poem as my eyes travel beyond your favorite window
in my room, and linger on the Irish stone,
marker of your remains in the courtyard of dry leaves
and nameless dampness.

You come in and out at will
when on nights of insomnia
you are my best companion,
you, my friend.

Luisa Futoransky y la gravedad

Los murciélagos son los únicos depositarios de ciertos misterios que por ser tan simples han tenido a toda la humanidad confundida por siglos. Ni Celestina, ni Coco Chanel, ni la Marquesa Borghese, ni mi madre Ada, a pesar de sus tan elegantes ardides químicos, pudieron nuncajamás ni podrán convertir arrugas en alas y detener el impacable paso del tiempo. Sólo los murciégalos tienen el secreto de la juventud.

Luisa Futoransky and Gravity

Bats are the sole possessors of certain mysteries that, because they are so simple, have baffled humanity for centuries. Not Celestina, not Coco Chanel, nor the Marquise of Borghese, not even my mother Ada, despite her ever so elegant chemical concoctions could ever change wrinkles into wings and halt the implacable flow of time. Only bats know the secret of youth.

De formas aerodinámicas y espejos de navegantes

Un buen viajero
no tiene ni planes precisos
ni la intención de llegar.

Lao Tsé

-Soñé que una vez un buitre llegó a mí volando.

No tratas de hacer realidad tus ideas,
sólo intentas vencer la resistencia del aire.
Te ocupas de imitar el vuelo de los pájaros
y vives en una casa que tiene guardavecinos,
y una aldaba, y un zaguán.

Como tantas casas de tu ciudad costera,
la mía, poco a poco, se sepulta bajo lava
y cenizas de una tiranía en erupción.

Leo el *Islario general de todas las islas del mundo*
de Alonso de Santa Cruz, cosmógrafo mayor
del rey Carlos I de España, y se me ocurren soluciones
para dudas e incógnitas.

-Sí, y me abrió la boca
y me pasó varias veces
sus plumas por ella.

Dédalo huyó de la isla de Creta
para escapar de la pena de muerte.
Olor a cuerpos descompuestos.
Aire que derrite cualquier cera.
Metamorfosis del alfarero que de
tanto no tener siente miedo

y cae al vacío de su propia nadez.

Combinas tus facultades de gran pintor
con las de constructor y mecánico.
Tus ciento sesenta hojas de garabatos
elijen sitios para edificar helicópteros y paracaídas,
para alzar el vuelo, para no tocar.

Pura imaginación la del Cosmógrafo de su Majestad,
que por ser judío, y además chueta, de esos conversos
de las Islas Baleares, teme atraerse las furias de la Iglesia.

-Sí, como queriendo insinuar
que durante toda mi vida
hablaría de alas.

Abre tu boca de nuevo, y en caso de que emane un ala,
intenta el vuelo.

Cualquier fantasía sirve para descubrir una ciudad
con palacios de piedra noble, sus iglesias, sus plazas rectangulares
llenas de frondosos árboles y flores, y sus calles, callejuelas y
avenidas batidas por la brisa del mar.

Evalúas la resistencia del aire, y la forma
aerodinámica te convence.

-Mi pequeño Leonardo es astuto y talentoso.
Ayer construyó una máquina de volar con
plumas de ganso atadas con cordones.

Son visibles los cordones que unen las alas artificiales
a los pies que han de impulsarlas.
Si suelto a los demonios sobre tu cuerpo,
se convierten en migajas de pan.

Ícaro parece que quisiera advertir
al osado niño del peligro de la empresa.

La palabra no pronunciable: escapar
La palabra soñada: escapar
La palabra maldita: escapar

La leyenda griega cuenta de piedras labradas,
de una bola de hilo, de una pasión que lo domina todo,
y de un agua propicia a las plumas.

Sin serrucho y sin torno el alfarero se desangra en una
página de un manuscrito donde aparecen dibujados
varios grifos atados al trono de Alejandro.

Y a la mañana siguiente el niño cuenta que leyó
un mensaje escueto que le trajo un ave:
"Ignorancia del que se atreve a gravitar".

De todas las leyendas de los tiempos antiguos,
la del osado vuelo, que celebra a la persona deseada,
y no deja medalla conmemorativa, es la que anuncia
que la vida continúa, que se han contado innumerables historias
acerca de hombres que se han elevado por los aires,
que la facultad de volar es cosa de diablos o de heréticos.

El niño escribe la palabra guardacantón en su cuaderno,
después añade la palabra esfera, después escupe sobre la hoja
y la tinta se vuelve un murciélago bajo unos dedos
que carecen de conocimientos, pero están llenos de insinuaciones.

Las goteras que destruyen nuestra casa
han dejado tallado un velero que impulsa la navegación aérea.
El aguafuerte atraviesa mares de nubes,
y un intento de lograr divertirnos,
gracias a las utopías de los inventores.

Of Aerodynamic Shapes and Navigators' Mirrors

A good traveler
has neither precise plans
nor any fixed destination.

Lao Tsu

"I dreamt that a vulture came flying towards me."

You don't try to make your ideas come true,
You just try to overcome the air's resistance.
You're busy imitating the birds in flight
and you live in a house that has wrought iron grilles,
and a latch on the door, and a foyer.

Like so many houses in your coastal city,
mine, little by little, is being buried under lava
and ashes of an erupting tyranny.

I read the *Compendium of All the World's Islands*
by Alonso de Santa Cruz, head cosmographer
to King Charles I of Spain, and I think of solutions
for resolving doubts and unknowns.

"Yes, and it opened my mouth
and brushed its feathers across it
several times."

Dedalus fled from the island of Crete
to escape the death penalty.
The reek of decomposing bodies.
Air that melts any kind of wax.
Metamorphosis of the potter who
from such want lives in fear

and falls into the vacuum of his own nothingness.

You combine your skills as a great painter
with those of builder and mechanic.
Your hundred and sixty scrawled pages
choose sites for the construction of helicopters and parachutes,
to soar into flight, beyond touch.

Pure imagination on the part of his Majesty's Cosmographer
who, because he is Jewish, and the son of conversos in
the Balearic Islands, fears attracting the furies of the Church.

> "Yes, as though wishing to insinuate
> that I'd talk about wings
> throughout my entire life."

Open your mouth again, and if a wing pokes out,
try to fly.

Any fantasy will serve to discover a city
with palaces of noble stone, its churches, its rectangular plazas
filled with leafy trees and flowers, and its streets, alleys and
avenues beaten by sea breezes.

You size up the air resistance, and the aerodynamic
shape convinces you.

> "My little Leonardo is bright and talented.
> Yesterday he built a flying machine
> with goose feathers tied on with cords."

I can see the cords that attach the artificial wings
to the feet that will propel them.
If I set loose the demons onto your body,
they will turn into crumbs of bread.

Icarus seems to want to alert
the daring child to the danger of his enterprise.

The unpronounceable word: escape
The coveted word: escape
The accursed word: escape

The Greek legend tells of etched stones,
of a ball of thread, of an all-controlling passion,
and of a special water of feathers.

Without hand-saw or wheel, the potter bleeds into
a manuscript page filled with drawings
of several griffins tied to Alexander's throne.

And the next morning, the boy tells of reading
a succinct message brought to him by a bird:
"Ignorance of the one who dares to gravitate."

Of all the legends of long gone times,
the one about the daring flight, that celebrates the desired person,
and awards no commemorative medal, is the one which announces
that life continues, that innumerable stories have been told
about men who have risen into the air,
that the ability to fly is an attribute of devils or of heretics.

The boy writes the word curbstone in his notebook,
then adds the word sphere, then spits on the page and the ink
spreads into a bat beneath fingers
that lack skills, but are filled with insinuations.

The dripping water that destroys our house
has carved out the outline of a sailing ship that encourages aerial navigation.
The etching crosses seas of clouds,
and attempts to amuse us,
thanks to the inventors' utopias.

Other Poetry Books by Carlota Caulfield

El tiempo es una mujer que espera. Madrid: Torremozas, 1986.

34th Street and other poems. Introduction by Jack Foley. San Francisco: Eboli Poetry Series, 1987.

Oscuridad divina. Madrid: Betania, 1987.

Angel Dust/Polvo de Angel/Polvere D'Angelo. Translated by Carol Maier, Pietro Civitareale, and the author. Madrid: Betania, 1990.

Oscurità divina. Translated by Rosella Livoli and Carlos Vitale. Pisa: Giardini Editori e Stampatori, 1990.

A las puertas del papel con amoroso fuego. Introduction by Marjorie Agosin. Madrid: Torremozas, 1996.

Autorretrato en ojo ajeno. Madrid: Betania, 2001.

At the Paper Gates with Burning Desire. Introduction by Marjorie Agosin. Translated by Angela McEwan and the author. Oakland: InteliBooks, 2001.

Movimientos metálicos para juguetes abandonados. Primer Premio Hispanoamericano de Poesía "Dulce María Loynaz" 2002. La Laguna, Tenerife: Gobierno de Canarias, 2003.

The Book of Giulio Camillo / El Libro de Giulio Camillo / Il Libro de Giulio Camillo. Oakland: InteliBooks, 2003. Introduction by John Goodby. Translated by Mary G. Berg, Pietro Civitareale, and the author.

Quincunce/Quincunx. Translated by Mary G. Berg and the author. Published as Special Book Supplement. *Puerto del Sol,* a semi-annual journal of the English Department of New Mexico State University, 2004.

Ticket to Ride. Essays & Poems. Oakland: Hurricane, an imprint of InteliBooks Publishers, 2005.

Chapbooks, Limited Editions

Fanaim. San Francisco: El Gato Tuerto, 1984.

Sometimes I Call Myself Childhood /A veces me llamo infancia. Miami-Boston: Solar, 1985.

Visual Games for Words & Sounds. Hyperpoems for the Macintosh. Diskette. San Francisco: Intelibooks, 1993.

Estrofas de papel, barro y tinta. Barcelona: Cafè Central, 1995.

Book of XXXIX Steps, a poetry game of discovery and imagination. Hyperbook for the Macintosh. 5 Diskettes. San Francisco: InteliBooks, 1995.
Libro de los XXXIX escalones/Libro dei XXXIX gradini. San Francisco-Venice, 1995. Translated by Pietro Civitareale. Limited edition of thirty-nine copies. Signed by the author.
Libro de los XXXIX escalones/Book of the XXXIX Steps. Tarzara, CA.: Luz Bilingual Publishing, 1997.
Book of the XXXIX Steps. A Poetry Game of Discovery and Imagination. CD-Rom for the Apple Macintosh. Oakland: InteliBooks, 1999.
Quincunce. Barcelona: Cafè Central, 2001.
Poemes. Memòria de la mirada. Translation to Catalan by Montserrat Abelló. Limited edition of twent-five copies designed by the Catalan artist Antònia Bové. Barcelona, 2004. Printed in the artist's studio.

The Author

Carlota Caulfield is a Cuban born poet of Irish descent. After many journeys that took her from Havana to Dublin to Havana to Zürich, New York, San Francisco, New Orleans, Mahón, Barcelona, Oakland and London, she currently makes her home between Berkeley, California and London, UK.

Caulfield is the author of eleven books of poems, including *34th Street and other poems, A las puertas del papel con amoroso fuego / At the Paper Gates with Burning Desire, The Book of Giulio Camillo. (A Model for a Theater of Memory), Quincunce/Quincunx* and *Ticket to Ride. Essays & Poems.*

Her work and translations has appeared in, among other publications, *Visions, Michigan Quarterly Review, The Texas Review, Haight Ashbury Literary Journal, Puente Libre, Nómada, Inti, AErea, Barcarola, Hostos Review, Tebot Bach, Textos* and *Poetry San Francisco.*

Among her awards are a Cintas Foundation Fellowship for Creative Writing (1987), the International Poetry Prize, "Ultimo Novecento" (Italy, 1988), Honorable Mention at the "Plural Prize" (Mexico City, 1993), Honorable Mention in the International Poetry Prize "Federico García Lorca," (Spain-USA-1994), the Italian International Poetry Prize "Riccardo Marchi-Torre di Calafuria," (1995), Honorable Mention for Poetry at the 1997 "Latino Writers Prize," sponsored by the Latin American Writers Institute of New York, and The First International Hispanic American Poetry Prize "Dulce María Loynaz" (Spain-Cuba, 2002).

Caulfield is Professor of Spanish and Spanish-American Studies at Mills College, Oakland, California.

Her HomePage is at <http://www.intelinet.org/Caulfield>

The Translator

Mary G. Berg is a Resident Scholar at the Women's Studies Research Center at Brandeis University. Her recent translations include poetry by Carlota Caulfield, Antonio Machado's *The Landscape of Castile* and *There is no Road: Proverbs* (both with Dennis Maloney), novels by Martha Rivera *(I've Forgotten Your Name)*, Laura Riesco (*Ximena at the Crossroads*), Libertad Demitropulos (*River of Sorrows*), three anthologies of recent stories by Cubans (*Open Your Eyes and Soar, New Cuban Fiction* and *Cuba on the Edge: Short Stories from the Island*), and texts gathered by Marjorie Agosín, including *Uncertain Travelers: Conversations with Jewish Women Immigrants to America* (Brandeis Series of Jewish Women) and *Taking Root: Narratives of Jewish Women in Latin America.*